ALSO BY DONALD JUSTICE

POETRY

New and Selected Poems   1995
A Donald Justice Reader   1991
The Sunset Maker   1987
Selected Poems   1979
Departures   1973
Night Light   1967
The Summer Anniversaries   1960

ESSAYS

Oblivion: On Writers and Writing   1998
Platonic Scripts   1984

EDITOR

Contemporary French Poetry (with Alexander Aspel)   1965
The Collected Poems of Weldon Kees   1960

COLLECTED POEMS

COLLECTED
POEMS

DONALD
JUSTICE

Alfred A. Knopf   New York   2006

Poems from the following previously published books are reprinted,
some in slightly different form, in this volume of *Collected Poems:*
The Summer Anniversaries, copyright © 1960, revised edition © 1981
by Donald Justice; published by Wesleyan University Press
Night Light, copyright © 1967, revised edition © 1981 by Donald
Justice; published by Wesleyan University Press
Departures, copyright © 1973 by Donald Justice; published by Atheneum
Selected Poems, copyright © 1979 by Donald Justice; published by Atheneum
The Sunset Maker, copyright © 1987 by Donald Justice; published by Atheneum
A Donald Justice Reader, copyright © 1991 by Donald Justice; published by
University Press of New England
New and Selected Poems, copyright © 1995 by Donald Justice; published by
Alfred A. Knopf

Grateful acknowledgment is made to the following publications in which
these poems first appeared, some in slightly different form:
The New Criterion: "Ralph: A Love Story"; "Couplets Concerning
Time"; "A Chapter in the Life of Mr. Kehoe, Fisherman"
The New Republic: "Epitaph for a Pair of Old Shoes"
The New Yorker: "School Letting Out"; "The Small White Churches of the Small
White Towns"; "There is a gold light in certain old paintings"
The Oxford American: "At the Young Composers' Concert"
Poetry: "The Voice of Col. von Stauffenberg Ascending Through
the Smoke and Dull Flames of Purgatory"
Solo IV: "Sonya sits at the piano, practicing"

Library of Congress Cataloging-in-Publication Data

Justice, Donald Rodney, 1925–
[Poems]
Collected poems / by Donald Justice.—1st ed.
p.   cm.
ISBN 0-375-71054-X (pbk)
I. Title.
PS3519.U825A6 2004
811'.54—dc22   2003065735

Manufactured in the United States of America
Published August 18, 2004
First paperback edition, May 2, 2006

To the memory
of my mother and father

Contents

DEPARTURES   (1973)

One

From SELECTED POEMS   (1979)

THE SUNSET MAKER (1987)

From NEW AND SELECTED POEMS (1995)

NEW POEMS

THE SUMMER ANNIVERSARIES

(1960)

TO JEAN

O recreate that hour
Divine Mnemosyne,
When all things to the eye
Their early splendors wore.

One

Anniversaries

Great Leo roared at my birth,
The windowpanes were lit
With stars' applausive light,
And I have heard that the earth
As far away as Japan
Was shaken again and again
The morning I came forth.
Many drew round me then,
Admiring. Beside my bed
The tall aunts prophesied,
And cousins from afar,
Predicting a great career.

At ten there came an hour
When, waking out of ether
Into an autumn weather
Inexpressibly dear,
I was wheeled superb in a chair
Past vacant lots in bloom
With goldenrod and with broom,
In secret proud of the scar
Dividing me from life,
Which I could admire like one
Come down from Mars or the moon,
Standing a little off.

By seventeen I had guessed
That the "really great loneliness"
Of James's governess

Might account for the ghost
On the other side of the lake.
Oh, all that year was lost
Somewhere among the black
Keys of Chopin! I sat
All afternoon after school,
Fingering his ripe heart,
While boys outside in the dirt
Kicked, up and down, their ball.

Thirty today, I saw
The trees flare briefly like
The candles upon a cake
As the sun went down the sky,
A momentary flash,
Yet there was time to wish
Before the light could die,
If I had known what to wish,
As once I must have known,
Bending above the clean,
Candlelit tablecloth
To blow them out with a breath.

Song

Morning opened
Like a rose,
And the snow on the roof
Rose-color took.
Oh, how the street
Toward light did leap!
And the lamps went out.
Brightness fell down
From the steeple clock
To the rows of shops
And rippled the bricks
Like the scales of a fish,
And all that day
Was a fairy tale
Told once in a while
To a good child.

To a Ten-Months' Child

for M.M.

Late arrival, no
One would think of blaming you
For hesitating so.

Who, setting his hand to knock
At a door so strange as this one,
Might not draw back?

Certainly, once admitted,
You will be made to feel
Like one of the invited.

Still, because you come
From so remote a kingdom,
You may feel out of place,

Tongue-tied and shy among
So many strangers, all
Babbling a strange tongue.

Well, that's no disgrace.
So might any person
So recently displaced,

Remembering the ocean,
So calm, so lately crossed.

The Poet at Seven

And on the porch, across the upturned chair,
The boy would spread a dingy counterpane
Against the length and majesty of the rain
And on all fours crawl in it like a bear,
To lick his wounds in secret, in his lair;
And afterward, in the windy yard again,
One hand cocked back, release his paper plane,
Frail as a mayfly to the faithless air.
And summer evenings he would spin around
Faster and faster till the drunken ground
Rose up to meet him, sometimes he would squat
Among the foul weeds of the vacant lot,
Waiting for dusk and someone dear to come
And whip him down the street, but gently, home.

The Snowfall

The classic landscapes of dreams are not
More pathless, though footprints leading nowhere
Would seem to prove that a people once
Survived for a little even here.

Fragments of a pathetic culture
Remain, the lost mittens of children,
And a single, bright, detasseled snow cap,
Evidence of some frantic migration.

The landmarks are gone. Nevertheless
There is something familiar about this country.
Slowly now we begin to recall

The terrible whispers of our elders
Falling softly about our ears
In childhood, never believed till now.

Landscape with Little Figures

There once were some pines, a canal, a piece of sky.
The pines are the houses now of the very poor,
Huddled together, in a blue, ragged wind.
Children go whistling their dogs, down by the mud flats,
Once the canal. There's a red ball lost in the weeds.
It's winter, it's after supper, it's goodbye.
O goodbye to the houses, the children, the little red ball,
And the pieces of sky that will go on now falling for days.

On the Death of Friends in Childhood

[handwritten annotation: eirie diction]

[handwritten annotation: not good or evil, innocent]

We shall not ever meet them bearded in heaven,
Nor sunning themselves among the bald of hell;
If anywhere, in the deserted schoolyard at twilight,
Forming a ring, perhaps, or joining hands
In games whose very names we have forgotten.
Come, memory, let us seek them there in the shadows.

[handwritten annotation: We've moved on, but they stay in childhood]

The Wall

for J.B.

The wall surrounding them they never saw;
The angels, often. Angels were as common
As birds or butterflies, but looked more human.
As long as the wings were furled, they felt no awe.
Beasts, too, were friendly. They could find no flaw
In all of Eden: this was the first omen.
The second was the dream which woke the woman.
She dreamed she saw the lion sharpen his claw.
As for the fruit, it had no taste at all.
They had been warned of what was bound to happen.
They had been told of something called the world.
They had been told and told about the wall.
They saw it now; the gate was standing open.
As they advanced, the giant wings unfurled.

A Dream Sestina

I woke by first light in a wood
Right in the shadow of a hill
And saw about me in a circle
Many I knew, the dear faces
Of some I recognized as friends.
I knew that I had lost my way.

I asked if any knew the way.
They stared at me like blocks of wood.
They turned their backs on me, those friends,
And struggled up the stubborn hill
Along that road which makes a circle.
No longer could I see their faces.

But there were trees with human faces.
Afraid, I ran a little way
But must have wandered in a circle.
I had not left that human wood;
I was no farther up the hill.
And all the while I heard my friends

Discussing me, but not like friends.
Through gaps in trees I glimpsed their faces.
(The trees grow crooked on that hill.)
Now all at once I saw the way—
Above a clearing in the wood
A lone bird wheeling in a circle,

And in that shadowed space the circle
Of those I thought of still as friends.

I drew near, calling, and the wood
Rang, and they turned their deaf faces
This way and that, but not my way.
They rose and danced upon the hill.

And it grew dark. Behind the hill
The sun slid down, a fiery circle.
Screeching, the bird flew on its way.
It was too dark to see my friends.
But then I saw them, and their faces
Were leaning above me like a wood.

Round me they circle on the hill.
But what is wrong with my friends' faces?
Why have they changed that way to wood?

Sestina on Six Words by Weldon Kees

I often wonder about the others,
Where they are bound for on the voyage,
What is the reason for their silence,
Was there some reason to go away?
It may be they carry a dark burden,
Expect some harm, or have done harm.

How can we show we mean no harm?
Approach them? But they shy from others.
Offer, perhaps, to share the burden?
They change the subject to the voyage,
Or turn abruptly, walk away,
To brood against the rail in silence.

What is defeated by their silence
More than love, less than harm?
Many already are looking their way,
Pretending not to. Eyes of others
Will follow them now the whole voyage
And add a little to the burden.

Others touch hands to ease the burden,
Or stroll, companionable in silence,
Counting the stars which bless the voyage,
But let the foghorn speak of harm,
Their hearts will stammer like the others',
Their hands seem in each other's way.

It is so obvious, in a way.
Each is alone, each with his burden.

To others they are always others,
And they can never break the silence,
Say, lightly, *thou,* but to their harm
Although they make many a voyage.

What do they wish for from the voyage
But to awaken far away
By miracle free from every harm,
Hearing at dawn that sweet burden
The birds cry after a long silence?
Where is that country not like others?

There is no way to ease the burden.
The voyage leads on from harm to harm,
A land of others and of silence.

Here in Katmandu

We have climbed the mountain.
There's nothing more to do.
It is terrible to come down
To the valley
Where, amidst many flowers,
One thinks of snow,

As, formerly, amidst snow,
Climbing the mountain,
One thought of flowers,
Tremulous, ruddy with dew,
In the valley.
One caught their scent coming down.

It is difficult to adjust, once down,
To the absence of snow.
Clear days, from the valley,
One looks up at the mountain.
What else is there to do?
Prayer wheels, flowers!

Let the flowers
Fade, the prayer wheels run down.
What have these to do
With us who have stood atop the snow
Atop the mountain,
Flags seen from the valley?

It might be possible to live in the valley,
To bury oneself among flowers,

If one could forget the mountain,
How, never once looking down,
Stiff, blinded with snow,
One knew what to do.

Meanwhile it is not easy here in Katmandu,
Especially when to the valley
That wind which means snow
Elsewhere, but here means flowers,
Comes down,
As soon it must, from the mountain.

The Metamorphosis

Past Mr. Raven's tavern
Up Cemetery Hill
Around by the Giant Oak
And Drowning Creek gone dry
Into the Hunting Woods
And that was how he went

At his back the wind
Blowing out of heaven
And at his feet foul weeds
That it was like to hell
And scarcely could he draw
Breath and the ribs did ache

No rest got under the oak
Nor water for the wound
Yet kept the way and drew
Home at length to haven
And the familiar hall
His key into the wards

Then owls cried out from the woods
And terrors of that ilk
So that the bitch at heel
A little moaned and whined
As she some fit were having
That back her long legs drew

Whereat his mouth stood dry
And without any words

Despite his heart heaving
And tongue working to speak
Some name to cast the wonder
Straight from his heart whole

Then bent he to the keyhole
Nor might his eyes withdraw
The while the hall unwound
That thing which afterwards
No man should know or its like
Whether dead or living

Southern Gothic

for W.E.B. & P.R.

Something of how the homing bee at dusk
Seems to inquire, perplexed, how there can be
No flowers here, not even withered stalks of flowers,
Conjures a garden where no garden is
And trellises too frail almost to bear
The memory of a rose, much less a rose.
Great oaks, more monumentally great oaks now
Than ever when the living rose was new,
Cast shade that is the more completely shade
Upon a house of broken windows merely
And empty nests up under broken eaves.
No damask any more prevents the moon,
But it unravels, peeling from a wall,
Red roses within roses within roses.

Sonnet to My Father

Father, since always now the death to come
Looks naked out from your eyes into mine,
Almost it seems the death to come is mine
And that I also shall be overcome,
Father, and call for breath when you succumb,
And struggle for your hand as you for mine
In hope of comfort that shall not be mine
Till for the last of me the angel come.
But, father, though with you in part I die
And glimpse beforehand that eternal place
Where we forget the pain that brought us there,
Father, and though you go before me there,
Leaving this likeness only in your place,
Yet while I live, you do not wholly die.

Beyond the Hunting Woods

I speak of that great house
Beyond the hunting woods,
Turreted and towered
In nineteenth-century style,
Where fireflies by the hundreds
Leap in the long grass,
Odor of jessamine
And roses, canker-bit,
Recalling famous times
When dame and maiden sipped
Sassafras or wild
Elderberry wine,
While far in the hunting woods
Men after their red hounds
Pursued the mythic beast.

I ask it of a stranger,
In all that great house finding
Not any living thing,
Or of the wind and the weather,
What charm was in that wine
That they should vanish so,
Ladies in their stiff
Bone and clean of limb,
And over the hunting woods
What mist had made them wild
That gentlemen should lose
Not only the beast in view
But Belle and Ginger too,
Nor home from the hunting woods
Ever, ever come?

Tales from a Family Album

How shall I speak of doom, and ours in special,
But as of something altogether common?
No house of Atreus ours, too humble surely,
The family tree a simple chinaberry
Such as springs up in Georgia in a season.
(Under it sags the farmer's broken wagon.)
Nor may I laud it much for shade or beauty,
Yet praise that tree for being prompt to flourish,
Spite of the worm and weather out of heaven.

I publish of my folk how they have prospered
With something in the eyes perhaps inherent,
Or great-winged nose, bespeaking an acquaintance,
Not casual and not recent, with a monster,
Citing, as an example of some courage,
That aunt, long gone, who kept one in a bird cage
Thirty-odd years in shape of a green parrot,
Nor overcame her fears, yet missed no feeding,
Thrust in the crumbs with thimbles on her fingers.

I had an uncle, long of arm and hairy,
Who seldom spoke in any lady's hearing
Lest that his tongue should light on aught unseemly,
Yet he could treat most kindly with us children
Touching that beast, wholly imaginary,
Which, hunting once, his hounds had got the wind of.
And even of this present generation
There is a cousin of no great removal
On whom the mark is printed of a forepaw.

How shall I speak of doom and not the shadow
Caught in the famished cheeks of those few beauties
My people boast of, being flushed and phthisic?
Of my own childhood I remember dimly
One who died young, though as a hag most toothless,
Her fine hair wintry, from a hard encounter
By moonlight in a dark wood with a stranger,
Who had as well been unicorn or centaur
For all she might recall of him thereafter.

There was a kinsman took up pen and paper
To write our history, whereat he perished,
Calling for water and the holy wafer,
Who had, till then, resisted much persuasion.
I pray your mercy on a leaf so shaken,
And mercy likewise on these other fallen,
Torn from the berry-tree in heaven's fashion,
That there was somewhat in their way of going
Put doom upon my tongue and bade me utter.

Two

Thus

As for the key, we know it must be minor.
B minor, then, as having passed for noble
On one or two occasions. As for the theme,
There being but the one, with variations,
Let it be spoken outright by the oboe
Without apology of any string,
But as a man speaks, openly, his heart
Among old friends, let this be spoken.
                                        Thus

The major resolution of the minor,
Johann's great signature, would be too noble.
It would do certain violence to our theme.
Therefore see to it that the variations
Keep faith with the plain statement of the oboe.
Entering quietly, let each chastened string
Repeat the lesson she must get by heart,
And without overmuch adornment.
                                        Thus.

Variations on a Theme from James

"large, loose, baggy monsters"

1

It's not a landscape from too near.
Like sorrows, they require some distance
Not to bulk larger than they are.
The risk is, backing off too far.
Once we have found a middle ground,
The warts, the pimples disappear.
There's but a shagginess remains,
An olive or a purple haze,
Which has at least that saving grace
Of average faces, average hills,
A nice, unshaven atmosphere.

2

Whatever goats are climbing there,
Being all invisible,
Animate objects of a will
Contemplative without desire,
Suffer no vertigo at all,
But climb until *our* spirits tire,
Or dine forever, or until
The speculative garbage fail,
Tin cans and comic books, which small,
Imaginary campers there
Forgot against this very hour.

3

Such art has nature in her kind
That in the shaping of a hill
She will take care to leave behind
Some few abutments here and there,
Something to cling to, just in case.
A taste more finical and nice
Would comb out kink and curl alike.
But O ye barbers at your trade,
What more beguiles us? Your coiffures?
Or gold come water falling down?

Ladies by Their Windows

1

They lean upon their windows. It is late.
Already it is twilight in their house;
Autumn is in their eyes. Twilit, autumnal—
Thus they regard themselves. What vanities!
As if all nature were a looking glass
To publish the small features of their ruin.

Each evening at their windows they arrive
As if in anticipation of farewells,
Though they would be still lingering if they could,
Weary, yet ever restless for the dance,
Old Cinderellas, hearing midnight strike,
The mouse-drawn coach impatient at the door.

2

The light in going still is golden, still
A single bird is singing in the wood,
Now one, now two, now three, and crickets start,
Bird-song and cricket-sigh; and all the small
Percussion of the grass booms as it can,
And chimes, and tinkles too, *fortissimo*.

It is the lurch and slur the world makes turning.
It is the sound of turning, of a wheel
Or hand-cranked grinder turning, though more pomp
To this, more fiery particles struck off
At each revolve; and the last turn reveals
The darker side of what was light before.

Six stars shine through the dark, and half a moon!
Night birds go spiralling upward with a flash
Of silvery underwings, silver ascendings,
The light of stars and of the moon their light,
And water lilies open to the moon,
The moon in wrinkles on the water's face.

To shine is to be surrounded by the dark,
To glimmer in the very going out,
As stars wink, sinking in the bath of dawn,
Or as a prong of moon prolongs the night—
Superfluous curve!—unused to brilliancies
Which pale her own, yet splurging all she has.

3

So ladies by their windows live and die.
It is a question if they live or die,
As in a stone-wrought frieze of beasts and birds
The question is, whether they go or stay.
It seems they stay, but rest is motion too,
As these old mimicries of stone imply.

Say, then, they go by staying, bird and beast,
Still gathering momentum out of calm,
Till even stillness seems too much of haste,
And haste too still. Say that they live by dying,
These who were warm and beautiful as summer,
Leaning upon their windows looking out,

Summer-surrounded then with leaf and vine,
With alternate sun and shade, these whom the noon
Wound once about with beauty and then unwound,
Whose warmth survives in coldness as of stone,
Beauty in shadows, action in lassitude,
Whose windows are the limits of their lives.

Women in Love

It always comes, and when it comes they know.
To will it is enough to bring them there.
The knack is this, to fasten and not let go.

Their limbs are charmed; they cannot stay or go.
Desire is limbo—they're unhappy there.
It always comes, and when it comes they know.

Their choice of hells would be the one they know.
Dante describes it, the wind circling there.
The knack is this, to fasten and not let go.

The wind carries them where they want to go,
Yet it seems cruel to strangers passing there.
It always comes, and when it comes they know
The knack is this, to fasten and not let go.

Love's Stratagems

But these maneuverings to avoid
The touching of hands,
These shifts to keep the eyes employed
On objects more or less neutral
(As honor, for the time being, commands)
Will hardly prevent their downfall.

Stronger medicines are needed.
Already they find
None of their stratagems have succeeded,
Nor would have, no,
Not had their eyes been stricken blind,
Hand cut off at the elbow.

A Map of Love

Your face more than others' faces
Maps the half-remembered places
I have come to while I slept—
Continents a dream had kept
Secret from all waking folk
Till to your face I awoke,
And remembered then the shore,
And the dark interior.

Speaking of Islands

You spoke of islands, where the fishing boats
Sleep by the docks like men beside their wives,
Content all night, while under them the waves,
Arching their backs a little, purr like cats
And rub against them peacefully. Some nights,
You said, nothing in all that harbor moves
Except those boats with motion of those waves
And a few sleepy gulls with cries like flutes.

You spoke of islands as I speak of you,
Sea-circled and remote, an island too,
And of such latitudes as islands keep,
And languorous airs, and fragrances offshore,
And blue approaches to desire and sleep,
O my belle harbor, my San Salvador!

Sonnet About P.

A woman I knew had seemed most beautiful
For being cold and difficult of access.
I saw my friend, the cleverest man of us,
But for a word from her to make him whole,
Himself fall speechless, like a boy at school,
And others also, followers of the chase,
Look up or down but not into that face,
Owing to the perfection of the skull.
I knew this lady a dozen years ago.
Since, that she has to two or three been kind,
After long siege, and these not of her sort,
And that she has both given and taken hurt,
Hearing all this, and more, I call to mind
That high, improbable bosom, which was snow.

Another Song

Merry the green, the green hill shall be merry.
Hungry, the owlet shall seek out the mouse,
And Jack his Joan, but they shall never marry.

And snow shall fly, the big flakes fat and furry.
Lonely, the traveler shall seek out the house,
And Jack his Joan, but they shall never marry.

Weary the soldiers go, and come back weary,
Up a green hill and down the withered hill,
And Jack from Joan, and they shall never marry.

In Bertram's Garden

Jane looks down at her organdy skirt,
As if *it* somehow were the thing disgraced,
For being there, on the floor, in the dirt,
And she catches it up about her waist,
Smooths it out along one hip,
And pulls it over the crumpled slip.

On the porch, green-shuttered, cool,
Asleep is Bertram, that bronze boy,
Who, having wound her around a spool,
Sends her spinning like a toy
Out to the garden, all alone,
To sit and weep on a bench of stone.

Soon the purple dark must bruise
Lily and bleeding heart and rose,
And the little Cupid lose
Eyes and ears and chin and nose,
And Jane lie down with others soon
Naked to the naked moon.

The Stray Dog by the Summerhouse

This morning, down
By the summerhouse,
I saw a stray,
A stray dog dead.
All white and brown
The dead friend lay,
All brown with a white
Mark on his head.
His eyes were bright
And open wide,
Bright, open eyes
With worms inside,
And the tongue hung loose
To the butterflies,
The butterflies
And the flying ants.

And because of the tongue
He seemed like one
Who has run too long,
And stops, and pants.
And because of the sun
There came a scent,
And it was strong.
It came and went
As if somewhere near
A round, ripe pear,
So ripe, so round,
Had dropped to the ground

And with the heat
Was turning black.
And the scent came back,
And it was sweet.

Anthony St. Blues

1

Morning. The roofs emerge, the yard—
Brown grass, puddled with snow, dog's bone—
Emerges slowly, but not yet
Her plumber from the widow's arms
To touch his dreaming truck awake
That all night slumbered by our curb,
Nor yet the lame child from his race,
His dog from rat and squirrel. Only,
At the horizon now, dark pines
Scatter their starlings to the wires.

2

Evening. The paper-boy on wheels
Turns at his corner into night.
The one-armed man, returning late,
Bends to retrieve the murderous news,
Tucks it beneath the willing stump,
And mounts once more with slippery care
The purgatory of the stoop.
Withindoors many now enact,
Behind drawn shades, their shadow lives.
The headlights, turning, grope their way.

A Winter Ode to the Old Men
of Lummus Park, Miami, Florida

Risen from rented rooms, old ghosts
Come back to haunt our parks by day,
They crept up Fifth Street through the crowd,
Unseeing and almost unseen,
Halting before the shops for breath,
Still proud, pretending to admire
The fat hens dressed and hung for flies
There, or perhaps the lone, dead fern
Dressing the window of a small
Hotel. Winter had blown them south—
How many? Twelve in Lummus Park
I counted, shivering where they stood,
A little thicket of thin trees,
And more on benches, turning with
The sun, wan heliotropes, all day.

O you who wear against the breast
The torturous flannel undervest
Winter and summer, yet are cold,
Poor cracked thermometers stuck now
At zero everlastingly,
Old men, bent like your walking sticks
As with the pressure of some hand,
Surely they must have thought you strong
To lean on you so hard, so long!

Counting the Mad

This one was put in a jacket,
This one was sent home,
This one was given bread and meat
But would eat none,
And this one cried No No No No
All day long.

This one looked at the window
As though it were a wall,
This one saw things that were not there,
This one things that were,
And this one cried No No No No
All day long.

This one thought himself a bird,
This one a dog,
And this one thought himself a man,
An ordinary man,
And cried and cried No No No No
All day long.

On a Painting by Patient B of the
Independence State Hospital for the Insane

1

These seven houses have learned to face one another,
But not at the expected angles. Those silly brown lumps,
That are probably meant for hills and not other houses,
After ages of being themselves, though naturally slow,
Are learning to be exclusive without offending.
The arches and entrances (down to the right out of sight)
Have mastered the lesson of remaining closed.
And even the skies keep a certain understandable distance,
For these are the houses of the very rich.

2

One sees their children playing with leopards, tamed
At great cost, or perhaps it is only other children,
For none of these objects is anything more than a spot,
And perhaps there are not any children but only leopards
Playing with leopards, and perhaps there are only the spots.
And the little maids that hang from the windows like tongues,
Calling the children in, admiring the leopards,
Are the dashes a child might represent motion by means of,
Or dazzlement possibly, the brilliance of solid-gold houses.

3

The clouds resemble those empty balloons in cartoons
Which approximate silence. These clouds, if clouds they are
(And not the smoke from the seven aspiring chimneys),
The more one studies them the more it appears
They too have expressions. One might almost say

They have their habits, their wrong opinions, that their
Impassivity masks an essentially lovable foolishness,
And they will be given names by those who live under them
Not public like mountains' but private like companions'.

To Satan in Heaven

Forgive, Satan, virtue's pedants, all such
As have broken our habits, or had none,
The keepers of promises, prizewinners,
Meek as leaves in the wind's circus, evenings;
Our simple wish to be elsewhere forgive,
Shy touchers of library atlases,
Envious of bird-flight, the whale's submersion;
And us forgive who have forgotten how,
The melancholy who, lacing a shoe,
Choose not to continue, the merely bored,
Who have modeled our lives after cloud-shapes;
For which confessing, have mercy on us,
The different and the indifferent,
In inverse proportion to our merit,
For we have affirmed thee secretly, by
Candle-glint in the polish of silver,
Between courses, murmured amenities,
Seen thee in mirrors by morning, shaving,
Or head in loose curls on the next pillow,
Reduced thee to our own scope and purpose,
Satan, who, though in heaven, downward yearned,
As the butterfly, weary of flowers,
Longs for the cocoon or the looping net.

From "BAD DREAMS" AND OTHER EARLY POEMS

(1948–1962)

Two Sonnets

ce monstre délicat

1 ON THE DEVIL IN OUR TIME

A dwarfish, pious, country kind of fool,
Much too big-hearted to be any use
Around the house, half cherishing abuse
For breaking every little household rule,
That servant, who'd break forty plates a day,
Out of anxiety to serve, no doubt,
Never again will follow us about:
Just as the preacher warned, he's run away.
Dull and unclean enough he was, but still
Not one of us had ever wished him ill.
Why, we had flowered to manhood in his care,
So used to him at last we'd stroke his hair!
He seemed in his own stubborn way above
Our wrath and God's, yet could not bear such love.

2 AN OLD-FASHIONED DEVIL

Who is it snarls our plow lines, wastes our fields,
Unbaits our hooks, and fishes out our streams?
Who leads our hunts to where the good earth yields
To marshlands, and we sink, but no one screams?
Who taught our children where the harlot lives?
They gnaw her nipples and they drain her pap,
Clapping their little hands like primitives,
With droll abandon bouncing on her lap.
Our wives may adore him; us he bores to tears.
Who cares if to our dry and yellowing grass
He strikes a match or two, then disappears?
It's only the devil on his flop-eared ass—
A beast too delicate to bear him well—
Come plodding by us on his way to hell.

summer 1948

51

The Return of Alcestis

HERCULES: I bring Alcestis from the dolorous shades.
ADMETUS: Ah, what can ail her, that she weeps nor smiles.
ALCESTIS: My latest sighs have somewhat scorched the veil.
Ah, what can ail me, that I weep nor smile?
Why hath he brought me from the dolorous shades?

1950

Autobiography

First was not,
Became a spot,
Then through and in
Felt heart begin,
And learning size
Nor needed eyes,
Yet colors grew
(Began with blue),
Nor ears yet felt
The silence melt,
Till wanting room
Broke through the womb,
From one with Mother
Became Another,
Began to cry
Am I! Am I!

1953

Two Songs from Don Juan in Hell

1   SGANARELLE'S SONG

The gardens are golden with leaves,
Notes drawn on the season's Exchange;
But my purse is as limp as the sleeves
That amputees learn to arrange.

    No, no, nothing assuages
    The pains of damnation
    Like regular wages
    And a two-weeks' vacation.

The sun and the moon are as bright
As coins that collectors collect.
But why should my purse be so light
With no sun for the moon to reflect?

    No, no, nothing assuages, etc.

2   DON JUAN'S SONG

The devil's like a jealous, jealous husband,
But I must blame his horns upon another.
Oh, evil's like a young wife from the country,
Approachable, but hardly worth the bother.

Damnation's like an heiress, much proposed to.
Why has she chosen me to be her groom?
Hell is a cheap hotel, if continental:
The bridal suite is just a small, hot room.

1953

The Metamorphoses of a Vampire

The woman, meanwhile, from her strawberry mouth—
Twisting and turning like a snake on coals,
And kneading her breasts against her corset-stays—
Let flow these words, all interfused with musk:
"My lips are moist; and I know how to make
A man forget all conscience deep in bed.
I dry all tears on my triumphant breasts
And set old men to laughing like young boys.
For those who see me naked and unveiled,
I take the place of sun, and moon, and stars!
I am, dear scholar, so well schooled in pleasure
That when I smother a man in my smooth arms
Or when I abandon to his teeth my bosom—
Shy and voluptuous, tender and robust—
Upon these cushions groaning with delight,
The impotent angels would damn themselves for me!"

When she had sucked the marrow from my bones,
And, languidly, I turned toward her intending
A love-kiss in return, I saw there only
A sort of leathery wineskin filled with pus!
I shut my eyes in a cold fright, and when
I opened them again to the good day,
Beside me lay no mannequin whose power
Seemed to have come from drinking human blood:
There trembled a confusion of old bones
Which creaked in turning like a weathervane,
Or like a signboard on an iron pole
Swung by the wind through the long winter nights.

translated from Baudelaire
1955

Monologue in an Attic

[*Enter* ARTHUR, *a man of about 30, through a trapdoor.*]
The sad aroma of mothballs—
What a beautiful smell that is!
But where can the flies have got to
Now, that used to buzz at the pane
All summer, making their music?
I used to sit here admiring
Those ridiculous, long-drawn-out
Wagnerian death agonies
Of theirs for hours; once in a while,
One might stand up and stretch his wings,
Revived like the heldentenor
By demands for an encore.

[*A buzzing of flies is heard.*]
                    Strange,
How nothing ever seems to change
Up here but the weather. Downstairs,
My mother's radio would be
Tuned to another opera.
Mother had tempests. Still, one could
Always escape to the attic. . . .

[speech from a play] c. 1958

56

From Bad Dreams

TIME: *mid-July, c. 1935*

PLACE: *the South*

CHORUS

Why do we turn in our beds,
Neither sleeping nor waking?

We have not heard any thunder.
We have not seen the lightning
Flash upon the horizon.
We have heard only the weathercock
Turning as usual, the clock
Wheezing before it strikes.
It is three o'clock in the morning.

Why do we turn in our beds,
Neither sleeping nor waking?

We should be used to the dark.
We should not mind so much
The absence of moonlight. We have only
To turn the light on again
To restore the shape of the attic.
We have only to wait for daybreak
To restore the fields to their places.

It is three o'clock in the morning.
We have not taken the journey
Of which, just now, we were dreaming.
We have not left, after all,
A world made more or less tolerable
By the addition of curtains
And photographs of the children.

We are the servants only,
To whom nothing much happens.

Soon shall be cockcrow. Soon
Shall be bird song under the rafters.
We shall descend the stairs
The back way, making no noise.
We shall perform the chores
To which we have grown accustomed.
We shall not lack for occupation.

An old man is dying
In another part of the house.

We can do nothing for him.
It does no good to remember
How, after the celebration,
Long after the children were sleeping,
He stood in the back yard pointing
The last of the Roman candles
Skyward, over the arbor.

An old man is dying
In another part of the house.
Why do we turn in our beds,
Neither sleeping nor waking?
We are the servants only.
We can do nothing for him.

Slowly now from their dreams the sleepers awaken.
    And as, slowly, they grow aware of the light,
Which only by very gradual stages invades their rooms,
    Timidly at first, testing the sill,
And then more boldly, crossing the floor, regarding itself
    Brightly in mirrors (which seem, indeed, to bloom,
Under such a gaze, like shy girls of the country,
    Or like small ponds that, dry all summer,
Brim all at once with the first rains of autumn)—
    It seems to them, half awake as they are,
That someone has left a light on for them,
    As a mother might for her children,
And that it has been burning there all night, quite close,
    Even while they were dreaming that they slept
In dark, comfortless rooms like these; or, in some cases, caves,
    Damp and airless; or a tunnel, extremely narrow,
Through which a train was expected momently, thundering.
    And the light left on seems to them perfectly natural,
And in fact necessary, for they have not yet remembered
    Who they are, and that they are no longer children.
And as, slowly now, they open their eyes to the light,
    It is in time to catch a glimpse of their dreams
Already disappearing around the last corner of sleep,
    The retreating tail of the monster winking and flashing.

Epilogue: To the Morning Light

O light,
Strike out across the pasture,
Where nightmare runs away now,
Unseating all her riders.
Show them the way through woods where
So recently they wandered,
Without direction. Shine, shine on those spiders'
Webs into which they blundered,
So many, recoiling with a gesture.

Dazzle the highways, paved
With fading journeys. And these walks
That lead into a town
From which the siege is lifting
Lace, lace with leaf-pattern now
Through the cooperation of the oaks
And a breeze constantly shifting.

Then leap the last gate lightly,
O prodigal. Approach
This house, this anxious house your nightly
Exile fills with such gloom. How many chores
Await you! It is to you these stories
Declare themselves, all three now,
And at your glance how whitely!

Peer in through the tinted oval
There where the stair turns. No longer
Delay your necessary arrival.
But quickly, quickly
Stoop to the frayed runner
And follow it up the stair—
Steep, but less dangerous now that you
Go with it everywhere.

Reward each sleeper
With waking, with forgetting,
Your brilliant trophies.
Raise them up, but with care,
From pallets, from sprung sofas,
Where they have hung suspended
Over abysms, chasms,
Or drifted deep and deeper
Down through lost, bottomless pools.
See that their dreams are ended.

Teach them to forgive the mirror
Its frank, unfaltering look,
And the sundial in the side yard
Its shadow, for your sake.
For only with your help shall
They come to see—and with no more
Than average daily terror—
All things for what they are,
All things for what they are.

1959

The Furies

One is a bitch with stinking
Fur matted with dung.
Kicked and pampered in turn,
Always it comes slinking
Bellywise after you
With damp muzzle, with tongue,
Beseeching some favor whose
Nature you never learn.
   This one is dangerous

Another rides your shoulder
Like any seaman's parrot,
Only its tongue is bolder.
No pet bird to be proud of,
It will rail and swear at
You seven days running out of
Mere avian pique
And rake at you with its beak.
   Some find this useful

The last resembles a mirror
With this one curious trick,
That it is blank always.
Where do you go then when you
Look therein? What hallways
Keep you? By what error
Is the great avenue
Suddenly emptied of its traffic?
   Avoid this one

for certain reviewers
1962

NIGHT LIGHT

(1967)

FOR NAT

The samovar has
Grown cold, the guitar
Wants tuning: Play, play!

Orpheus Opens His Morning Mail

Bills. Bills. From the mapmakers of hell, the repairers of fractured
lutes, the bribed judges of musical contests, etc.

A note addressed to my wife, marked: *Please Forward.*

A group photograph, signed: *Your Admirers.* In their faces a certain
sameness, as if "1" might, after all, be raised to some modest
power; likewise in their costumes, at once transparent and
identical, like those of young ladies at some debauched
seminary. Already—such is my weakness—I picture the rooms
into which they must once have locked themselves to read my
work: those barren cells, beds ostentatiously unmade; the
single pinched chrysanthemum, memorializing in a corner
some withered event; the mullioned panes, high up, through
which may be spied, far off, the shorn hedge behind which a
pimply tomorrow crouches, exposing himself. O lassitudes!

Finally, an invitation to attend certain rites to be celebrated, come
equinox, on the river bank. I am to be guest of honor. As
always, I rehearse the scene in advance: the dark; the guards,
tipsy as usual, sonorously snoring; a rustling, suddenly, among
the reeds; the fitful illumination of ankles, whitely flashing . . .
Afterwards, I shall probably be asked to recite my poems. But
O my visions, my vertigoes! Have I imagined it only, the
perverse gentility of their shrieks?

Time and the Weather

Time and the weather wear away
The houses that our fathers built.
Their ghostly furniture remains—
All the sad sofas we have stained
With tears of boredom or of guilt,

The fraying mottoes, the stopped clocks . . .
And still sometimes these tired shapes
Haunt the damp parlors of the heart.
What Sunday prisons they recall!
And what miraculous escapes!

To the Unknown Lady Who Wrote the Letters Found in the Hatbox

*To be sold at auction. . . . 1 brass bed, 1 walnut
secretary . . . bird cages, a hatbox of old letters . . .*
— NEWSPAPER ADVERTISEMENT

What, was there never any news?
And were your weathers always fine,
Your colds all common, and your blues
Too minor to deserve one line?

Between the lines it must have hurt
To see the neighborhood go down,
Your neighbor in his undershirt
At dusk come out to mow his lawn.

But whom to turn to to complain,
Unless it might be your canaries,
And only in bird language then?
While slowly into mortuaries

The many-storied houses went
Or in deep, cataracted eyes
Displayed their signs of want: FOR RENT
And MADAM ROXIE WILL ADVISE.

The Grandfathers

Why will they never sleep?
—JOHN PEALE BISHOP

Why will they never sleep,
The old ones, the grandfathers?
Always you find them sitting
On ruined porches, deep
In the back country, at dusk,
Hawking and spitting.
They might have sat there forever,
Tapping their sticks,
Peevish, discredited gods.
Ask of the traveler how,
At road-end, they will fix
You maybe with the cold
Eye of a snake or a bird
And answer not a word,
Only these blank, oracular
Head-shakes or head-nods.

Dreams of Water

An odd silence
Falls as we enter
The cozy ship's-bar.

The captain, smiling,
Unfolds his spyglass
And offers to show you

The obscene shapes
Of certain islands,
Low in the offing.

I sit by in silence.

People in raincoats
Stand looking out from
Ends of piers.

A fog gathers;
And little tugs,
Growing uncertain

Of their position,
Start to complain
With the deep and bearded

Voices of fathers.

3

The season is ending.
White verandas
Curve away.

The hotel seems empty
But, once inside,
I hear a great splashing.

Behind doors
Grandfathers loll
In steaming tubs,

Huge, unblushing.

Ode to a Dressmaker's Dummy

*Papier-mâché body; blue-and-black
cotton jersey cover. Metal stand.
Instructions included.*
—SEARS, ROEBUCK CATALOGUE

O my coy darling, still
You wear for me the scent
Of those long afternoons we spent,
The two of us together,
Safe in the attic from the jealous eyes
Of household spies
And the remote buffooneries of the weather;
So high,
Our sole remaining neighbor was the sky,
Who, often enough, at dusk,
Leaning her cloudy shoulders on the sill,
Used to regard us with a bored and cynical eye.

How like the terrified,
Shy figure of a bride
You stood there then, without your clothes,
Drawn up into
So classic and so strict a pose
Almost, it seemed, the little attic grew
Dark with the first charmed night of the honeymoon.
Or was it only some obscure
Shape of my mother's youth I saw in you,
There where the rude shadows of the afternoon
Crept up your ankles and you stood
Hiding your sex as best you could?—
Prim ghost the evening light shone through.

Memory of a Porch

Miami, 1942

What I remember
Is how the wind chime
Commenced to stir
As she spoke of her childhood,

As though the simple
Death of a pet cat,
Buried with flowers,

Had brought to the porch
A rumor of storms
Dying out over
Some dark Atlantic.

At least I heard
The thing begin—
A thin, skeletal music—

And in the deep silence
Below all memory
The sighing of ferns
Half asleep in their boxes.

But That Is Another Story

I do not think the ending can be right.
How can they marry and live happily
Forever, these who were so passionate
At chapter's end? Once they are settled in
The quiet country house, what will they do,
So many miles from anywhere?
Those blond ancestral ghosts crowding the stair,
Surely they disapprove? Ah me,
I fear love will catch cold and die
From pacing naked through those drafty halls
Night after night. Poor Frank! Poor Imogene!
Before them now their lives
Stretch empty as great Empire beds
After the lovers rise and the damp sheets
Are stripped by envious chambermaids.

And if the first night passes brightly enough,
What with the bonfires lit with old love letters,
That is no inexhaustible fuel, perhaps?
God knows how it must end, not I.
Will Frank walk out one day
Alone through the ruined orchard with his stick,
Strewing the path with lissome heads
Of buttercups? Will Imogene
Conceal in the crotches of old trees
Love notes for beardless gardeners and such?
Meanwhile they quarrel and make it up
Only to quarrel again. A sudden storm
Pulls the last fences down. Now moonstruck sheep
Stray through the garden all night peering in
At the exhausted lovers where they sleep.

Heart

Heart, let us this once reason together.
Thou art a child no longer. Only think
What sport the neighbors have from us, not without cause.
These nightly sulks, these clamorous demonstrations!
Already they tell of thee a famous story.
An antique, balding spectacle such as thou art,
Affecting still that childish, engaging stammer
With all the seedy innocence of an overripe pomegranate!
Henceforth, let us conduct ourselves more becomingly!

And still I hear thee, beating thy little fist
Against the walls. My dear, have I not led thee,
Dawn after streaky dawn, besotted, home?
And still these threats to have off as before?
From thee, who wouldst lose thyself in the next street?
Go then, O my inseparable, this once more.
Afterwards we will take thought for our good name.

Girl Sitting Alone at Party

You sit with hands folded—
A madonna, a rock.

And yet when your eyes move,
As they do,

As they cannot help doing,
Your eyes are dancers.

It is for them that the rooms below
Were darkened.

And when you go,
It is there, toward music.

Your shadow, though,
Stays with me.

It sits with hands folded, stubbornly.
It will say nothing.

It is a dark rock
Against which the sea beats.

This is that other music, to which
I embrace your shadow.

Party

After midnight the charm
Begins to seem less potent,
And still the little band of initiates

Stand about in their circle
Attempting the ancient modes
Lord Bacchus himself must have invented.

If so far they have failed
To summon up any but the
Familiar demons of a banal whimsy,

Let us not imagine
That the invisible ones
Are either innocent or ignorable.

Even now as we go on
Pretending to pay them only
The politer forms of inattention,

Leer and Pinch Me and their kind
Are taking possession of
Our crowded rooms, our empty persons.

A Local Storm

The first whimper of the storm
At the back door, wanting in,
Promised no such brave creature
As threatens now to perform
Black rites of the witch Nature
Publicly on our garden.

Thrice he has circled the house
Murmuring incantations,
Doing a sort of war dance.
Does he think to frighten us
With his so primitive chants
Or merely try our patience?

The danger lies, after all,
In being led to suppose—
With Lear—that the wind dragons
Have been let loose to settle
Some private grudge of heaven's.
Still, how nice for our egos.

Variations for Two Pianos

for Thomas Higgins, pianist

There is no music now in all Arkansas.
Higgins is gone, taking both his pianos.

Movers dismantled the instruments, away
Sped the vans. The first detour untuned the strings.

There is no music now in all Arkansas.

Up Main Street, past the cold shopfronts of Conway,
The brash, self-important brick of the college,

Higgins is gone, taking both his pianos.

Warm evenings, the windows open, he would play
Something of Mozart's for his pupils, the birds.

There is no music now in all Arkansas.

How shall the mockingbird mend her trill, the jay
His eccentric attack, lacking a teacher?

Higgins is gone, taking both his pianos.
There is no music now in all Arkansas.

Anonymous Drawing

A delicate young Negro stands
With the reins of a horse clutched loosely in his hands;
So delicate, indeed, that we wonder if he can hold the spirited
    creature beside him
Until the master shall arrive to ride him.
Already the animal's nostrils widen with rage or fear.
But if we imagine him snorting, about to rear,
This boy, who should know about such things better than we,
Only stands smiling, passive and ornamental, in a fantastic livery
Of ruffles and puffed breeches,
Watching the artist, apparently, as he sketches.
Meanwhile the petty lord who must have paid
For the artist's trip up from Perugia, for the horse, for the boy, for
    everything here, in fact, has been delayed,
Kept too long by his steward, perhaps, discussing
Some business concerning the estate, or fussing
Over the details of his impeccable toilet
With a manservant whose opinion is that any alteration at all
    would spoil it.
However fast he should come hurrying now
Over this vast greensward, mopping his brow
Clear of the sweat of the fine Renaissance morning, it would be
    too late:
The artist will have had his revenge for being made to wait,
A revenge not only necessary but right and clever—
Simply to leave him out of the scene forever.

To Waken a Small Person

You sleep at the top of streets
Up which workmen each morning
Go wheeling their bicycles

Your eyes are like the windows
Of some high attic the one
The very one you sleep in

They're shut it's raining the rain
Falls on the streets of the town
As it falls falls through your sleep

You must be dreaming these tears
Wake up please open yourself
Like a little umbrella

Hurry the sidewalks need you
The awnings not one is up
And the patient bicycles

Halted at intersections
They need you they are confused
The colors of traffic lights

Are bleeding bleeding wake up
The puddles of parking lots
Cannot contain such rainbows

American Sketches

CROSSING KANSAS BY TRAIN

The telephone poles
Have been holding their
Arms out
A long time now
To birds
That will not
Settle there
But pass with
Strange cawings
Westward to
Where dark trees
Gather about a
Water hole this
Is Kansas the
Mountains start here
Just behind
The closed eyes
Of a farmer's
Sons asleep
In their work clothes

POEM TO BE READ AT 3 A.M.

Excepting the diner
On the outskirts
The town of Ladora
At 3 a.m.
Was dark but
For my headlights
And up in
One second-story room
A single light
Where someone
Was sick or
Perhaps reading
As I drove past
At seventy
Not thinking
This poem
Is for whoever
Had the light on

After a Phrase Abandoned by Wallace Stevens

The alp at the end of the street
—STEVENS' NOTEBOOKS

The alp at the end of the street
Occurs in the dreams of the town.
Over burgher and shopkeeper,
Massive, he broods,
A snowy-headed father
Upon whose knees his children
No longer climb;
Or is reflected
In the cool, unruffled lakes of
Their minds, at evening,
After their day in the shops,
As shadow only, shapeless
As a wind that has stopped blowing.

Grandeur, it seems,
Comes down to this in the end—
A street of shops
With white shutters
Open for business . . .

Elsewheres

SOUTH

The long green shutters are drawn.
Against what parades?

Closing our eyes against the sun,
We try to imagine

The darkness of an interior
In which something might still happen:

The razor lying open
On the cool marble washstand,

The drip of something—is it water?—
Upon stone floors.

NORTH

Already it is midsummer
In the Sweden of our lives.

The peasants have joined hands,
They are circling the haystacks.

We watch from the veranda.
We sit, mufflered,

Humming the tune in snatches
Under our breath.

We tremble sometimes,
Not with emotion.

WAITING ROOM

Reading the signs,
We learn what to expect—

The trains late,
The machines out of order.

We learn what it is
To stare out into space.

Great farms surround us,
Squares of a checkerboard.

Taking our places, we wait,
We wait to be moved.

Men at Forty

Men at forty
Learn to close softly
The doors to rooms they will not be
Coming back to.

At rest on a stair landing,
They feel it moving
Beneath them now like the deck of a ship,
Though the swell is gentle.

And deep in mirrors
They rediscover
The face of the boy as he practices tying
His father's tie there in secret,

And the face of that father,
Still warm with the mystery of lather.
They are more fathers than sons themselves now.
Something is filling them, something

That is like the twilight sound
Of the crickets, immense,
Filling the woods at the foot of the slope
Behind their mortgaged houses.

Early Poems

How fashionably sad those early poems are!
On their clipped lawns and hedges the snows fall.
Rains beat against the tarpaulines of their porches,
Where, Sunday mornings, the bored children sprawl,
Reading the comics before their parents rise.
—The rhymes, the meters, how they paralyze!

Who walks out through their streets tonight? No one.
You know these small towns, how all traffic stops
At ten, the corner street lamps gathering moths,
And mute, pale mannequins waiting in dark shops,
Undressed, and ready for the dreams of men.
—Now the long silence. Now the beginning again.

The Thin Man

I indulge myself
In rich refusals.
Nothing suffices.

I hone myself to
This edge. Asleep, I
Am a horizon.

The Missing Person

He has come to report himself
A missing person.

The authorities
Hand him the forms.

He knows how they have waited
With the learned patience of barbers

In small shops, idle,
Stropping their razors.

But now that these spaces in his life
Stare up at him blankly,

Waiting to be filled in,
He does not know how to begin.

Afraid that he may not answer even
To his description of himself,

He asks for a mirror.
They reassure him

That he can be nowhere
But wherever he finds himself

From moment to moment,
Which, for the moment, is here.

And he might like to believe them.
But in the mirror

He sees what is missing.
It is himself

He sees there emerging
Slowly, as from the dark

Of a furnished room
Only by darkness,

One who receives no mail
And is known to the landlady only

For keeping himself to himself,
And for whom it will be years yet

Before he can trust to the light
This last disguise, himself.

The Man Closing Up

improvisations on themes from Guillevic

1

Like a deserted beach,
The man closing up.

Broken glass on the rocks,
And seaweed coming in
To hang up on the rocks.

Old pilings, rotted, broken like teeth,
Where a pier was,

A mouth,
And the tide coming in.

The man closing up
Is like this.

2

He has no hunger
For anything,
The man closing up.

He would even try stones,
If they were offered.

But he has no hunger
For stones.

3

He would make his bed,
If he could sleep on it.

He would make his bed with white sheets
And disappear into the white,

Like a man diving,
If he could be certain

That the light
Would not keep him awake,

The light that reaches
To the bottom.

4

The man closing up
Tries the doors.

But first
He closes the windows.

And before that even
He had looked out the windows.

There was no storm coming
That he could see.

There was no one out walking
At that hour.

Still,
He closes the windows
And tries the doors.

He knows about storms
And about people

And about hours
Like that one.

5

There is a word for it,
A simple word,
And the word goes around.

It curves like a staircase,
And it goes up like a staircase,
And it *is* a staircase,

An iron staircase
On the side of a lighthouse.
All in his head.

And it makes no sound at all
In his head,
Unless he says it.

Then the keeper
Steps on the rung,
The bottom rung,

And the ascent begins.
Clangorous,
Rung after rung.

He wants to keep the light going,
If he can.

But the man closing up
Does not say the word.

Hands

Les mains ne trouvaient plus
De bonheur dans les poches.
— GUILLEVIC

No longer do the hands know
The happiness of pockets.

Sometimes they hang at the sides
Like the dead weights of a clock.

Sometimes they clench into fists
Around the neck of anger.

Formerly there were brothers
To clasp, shoulders to rest on.

If now they unfold like maps,
All their countries seem foreign.

They dream of returning to
The dark home of the pockets.

They want to wash themselves clean
Of the blood of old salutes,

To scrub away the perfumes
Of the flesh they have tasted.

And all that they grasp is air.
Think of the hands as breathing,

Opening, closing. Think of
The emptiness of the hands.

The Evening of the Mind

Now comes the evening of the mind.
Here are the fireflies twitching in the blood;
Here is the shadow moving down the page
Where you sit reading by the garden wall.
Now the dwarf peach trees, nailed to their trellises,
Shudder and droop. You know their voices now,
Faintly the martyred peaches crying out
Your name, the name nobody knows but you.
It is the aura and the coming on.
It is the thing descending, circling, here.
And now it puts a claw out and you take it.
Thankfully in your lap you take it, so.

You said you would not go away again,
You did not want to go away—and yet,
It is as if you stood out on the dock
Watching a little boat drift out
Beyond the sawgrass shallows, the dead fish . . .
And you were in it, skimming past old snags,
Beyond, beyond, under a brazen sky
As soundless as a gong before it's struck—
Suspended how?—and now they strike it, now
The ether dream of five-years-old repeats, repeats,
And you must wake again to your own blood
And empty spaces in the throat.

For the Suicides of 1962

in memory: J. & G.

If we recall your voices
As softer now, it's only
That they must have drifted back

A long way to have reached us
Here, and upon such a wind
As crosses the high passes.

Nor does the blue of your eyes
(Remembered) cast much light on
The page ripped from the tablet.

                    *

Once there in the labyrinth,
You were safe from your reasons.
We stand, now, at the threshold,

Peering in, but the passage,
For us, remains obscure; the
Corridors are still bloody.

                    *

What you meant to prove you have
Proved: we did not care for you
Nearly enough. Meanwhile the

Bay was preparing herself
To receive you, the for once
Wholly adequate female

To your dark inclinations;
Under your care the pistol
Was slowly learning to flower

In the desired explosion,
Disturbing the careful part
And the briefly recovered

Fixed smile of a forgotten
Triumph; deep within the black
Forest of childhood that tree

Was already rising which,
With the length of your body,
Would cast the double shadow.

*

The masks by which we knew you
Have been torn from you. Even
Those mirrors, to which always

You must have turned to confide,
Cannot have recognized you,
Stripped, as you were, finally.

At the end of your shadow
There sat another, waiting,
Whose back was always to us.

*

When the last door had been closed,
You watched, inwardly raging,
For the first glimpse of your selves
Approaching, jangling their keys.

Musicians of the black keys,
At last you compose yourselves.
We hear the music raging
Under the lids we have closed.

The Tourist from Syracuse

You would not recognize me.
Mine is the face which blooms in
The dank mirrors of washrooms
As you grope for the light switch.

My eyes have the expression
Of the cold eyes of statues
Watching their pigeons return
From the feed you have scattered,

And I stand on my corner
With the same marble patience.
If I move at all, it is
At the same pace precisely

As the shade of the awning
Under which I stand waiting
And with whose blackness it seems
I am already blended.

I speak seldom, and always
In a murmur as quiet
As that of crowds which surround
The victims of accidents.

Shall I confess who I am?
My name is all names and none.
I am the used-car salesman,
The tourist from Syracuse,

The hired assassin, waiting.
I will stand here forever
Like one who has missed his bus—
Familiar, anonymous—

On my usual corner,
The corner at which you turn
To approach that place where now
You must not hope to arrive.

Bus Stop

Lights are burning
In quiet rooms
Where lives go on
Resembling ours.

The quiet lives
That follow us—
These lives we lead
But do not own—

Stand in the rain
So quietly
When we are gone,
So quietly . . .

And the last bus
Comes letting dark
Umbrellas out—
Black flowers, black flowers.

And lives go on.
And lives go on
Like sudden lights
At street corners

Or like the lights
In quiet rooms
Left on for hours,
Burning, burning.

Incident in a Rose Garden

a variation on an old theme
for Mark Strand

GARDENER: Sir, I encountered Death
                Just now among our roses.
                Thin as a scythe he stood there.

                I knew him by his pictures.
                He had his black coat on,
                Black gloves, a broad black hat.

                I think he would have spoken,
                Seeing his mouth stood open.
                Big it was, with white teeth.

                As soon as he beckoned, I ran.
                I ran until I found you.
                Sir, I am quitting my job.

                I want to see my sons
                Once more before I die.
                I want to see California.

MASTER: Sir, you must be that stranger
                Who threatened my gardener.
                This is my property, sir.

                I welcome only friends here.
DEATH: Sir, I knew your father,
                And we were friends at the end.

As for your gardener,
I did not threaten him.
Old men mistake my gestures.

I only meant to ask him
To show me to his master.
I take it you are he?

In the Greenroom

How reassuring
To discover them
In the greenroom. Here,

Relaxing, they drop
The patronymics
By which we had come

To know them. The cross
Are no longer cross,
The old dance, nor have

The young sacrificed
Their advantages.
In this it is like

A kind of heaven
They rise to simply
By being themselves.

The sound of the axe
Biting the wood is
Rewound on the tape.

What is this green for
If not renewal?

At a Rehearsal of "Uncle Vanya"

NURSE: *The crows might get them.*

You mean well, doctor,
But are—forgive me—
A bit of a crank,

A friend they may love
But cannot listen
To long, for yawning.

When you are gone, though,
They move up close to
The stove's great belly.

Yes, they are burning
Your forests, doctor,
The dark green forests.

There is a silence
That falls between them
Like snow, like deep snow.

Horses have gone lame
Crossing the wastelands
Between two people.

Doctor, who is well?
Leaning out across
Our own distances,

We hear the old nurse
Calling her chickens
In now: *chook chook chook.*

It's cold in Russia.
We sit here, doctor,
In the crows' shadow.

San Francisco, Actor's Workshop,
December, 1964

Last Days of Prospero

The aging magician retired to his island.
It was not so green as he remembered,
Nor did the sea caress its headlands
With the customary nuptial music.

He did not mind. He would not mind,
So long as the causeway to the mainland
Were not repaired, so long as the gay
Little tourist steamer never again

Lurched late into harbor, and no one
Applied for a license to reopen
The shuttered, gilt casino. Better,
He thought, an isle unvisited

Except for the sea birds come to roost
On the roofs of the thousand ruined cabañas,
Survivors; or the strayed whale, offshore,
Suspicious, surfacing to spout,

Noble as any fountain of Mílan . . .
The cave? That was as he had left it,
Amply provisioned against the days
To come. His cloak? Neat on its hanger.

The painted constellations, though faded
With damp a little, still glittered
And seemed in the dark to move on course.
His books? He knew where they were drowned.

(What tempests he had caused, what lightnings
Loosed in the rigging of the world!)
If now it was all to do again,
Nothing was lacking to his purpose.

Some change in the wording of the charm,
Some slight reshuffling of negative
And verb, perhaps: that should suffice.
So, so. Meanwhile he paced the strand,

Debating, as old men will, with himself
Or the waves, and still the waves kept coming
Back at him always with the same
Low chucklings or grand, indifferent sighs.

Memo from the Desk of X

Re: the question of poems.
Certainly your proposal
Merits consideration.

I myself recall fondly
Old friends among the poems—
Harmless, but to what purpose?

Some few indeed we might keep
Alive, in transparent tents,
As an example to youth

Of the great waste the past was.
The white face of a poem
Turned to the wall, the almost

Visible heartbeat, the deep
But irregular breathing—
No harm to the state in this.

The average citizen
Might be the healthier for
Some such exposure. Granted.

Nevertheless, we must weigh
The cost against the result.
Aside from supervision,

Frequent transfusions of blood—
And often of some rare type—
Would have to be provided,

And guides trained to interpret
Their curious expressions
For the new generation,

Those who have had no chance to
Learn much about suffering.
We of an older order

Should be prepared to refute
All charges of nostalgia.
We must look to the future.

I am told by our experts
That an esthetic response
To straight lines and to circles

May be acquired, with study.
This strikes me as promising.
Our landscapes already are

Shifting in that direction;
Likewise our lives. This approach
Is not unrealistic.

I therefore must recommend,
Though not without some regret,
The extinction of poems.

For a Freshman Reader

after the German of Hans Magnus Enzensberger

Don't bother with odes, my son.
Timetables are more precise.

Currents are changing. Unroll
The sea charts. Watch it, don't sing.

The day will come when once more
Lists will be nailed to the door

And numbers stamped on the chest
Of anyone who says No.

Learn to be anonymous,
Learn more than I did: to change

Your identification,
Your address, your appearance.

Encyclicals make good fires,
Manifestos are handy

For wrapping up the butter
And salt given to victims.

It will take more than anger,
It will take patience to force

The lungs of authority
With the fine deadly powder

Ground by those with the know-how,
The precisionists, like you.

To the Hawks

McNamara, Rusk, Bundy

Farewell is the bell
Beginning to ring.

The children singing
Do not yet hear it.

The sun is shining
In their song. The sun

Is in fact shining
Upon the schoolyard,

On children swinging
Like tongues of a bell

Swung out on the long
Arc of a silence

That will not seem to
Have been a silence

Till it is broken,
As it is breaking.

There is a sun now
Louder than the sun

Of which the children
Are singing, brighter,

Too, than that other
Against whose brightness

Their eyes seem caught in
The act of shutting.

The young schoolteacher,
Waving one arm in

Time to the music,
Is waving farewell.

Her mouth is open
To sound the alarm.

The mouth of the world
Grows round with the sound.

February, 1965

Poem for a Survivor

for R.G.S.

Holding this poem
Close, like a mirror,
I breathe upon it.

I watch for some sign.
There is a faint mist
Spreading across it.

It takes hold. It clings
To the lean hollows
As the sun rises,

This sun that is going
To burn the mist off.

I give you chamois
To clear the surface.

I give you this sun.

Narcissus at Home

A room composed entirely of mirrors. NARCISSUS, *on a divan, a simple hand mirror clutched to his bosom, into which he gazes languidly from time to time.*

Alone at last! But I am forgetting myself . . .

To that other—to him I imagine crouched on the far side of the glass, that spy, condemned forever to his vain search for the promised peephole—to him, indeed, it might appear that I was alone.

But you and I, my dear, know better.

Only you can guess what comfort it brings me to see you in there, ever agreeable, nodding your head just as I nod mine—and which of us greets the other first, who shall say?

And you as well. And you.

Here, if anywhere, one might be content:

To be surrounded always by what one loves best in all the world; to see, wherever one turns, that single prospect which most allures the eye:

Like the distant view of a sea so tempting that one could imagine drowning oneself there with pleasure:

Granted, an incomparable view.

Yet can it be possible to bear so much beauty without some taint of suffering?

Even to one set apart like me, the bad days come, the times when I, like the rest, begin to doubt myself.

To have fallen in love with a simple hand mirror, amidst such a multitude at first glance so much more impressive, does that not in itself suggest that I may think of myself in rather humble terms, after all? That I may regard myself as less than handsome?

Is it conceivable?

Yes, the evidence is unmistakable: no change since the last glimpse I stole.

Never a change, never any improvement, despite this succession of tedious creams, these ointments smuggled in from the Orient, and at such cost.

If anything, a particle of deterioration. Just here, about the eyes, I should say. Yes, admittedly, a trifle wearier.

Not that I would think of blaming you, my eyes, you who have such prodigies of labor to perform, constantly peering and gazing. Will you never be still?

If, then, as it seems, I shall be obliged in the future to consider myself, in plain truth, not much above the average in appearance, that is no doubt because I am denied the privilege of seeing myself as others see me.

No longer should I be amazed when others regard me with wonder. I must learn to accustom myself to their sighs, their exclamations, those spontaneous bursts of applause which have always somewhat embarrassed me:

Admirers of beauty, I understand them now. There can be but the one explanation. The mirror reverses the image!

How shocked they would be if they could divine my secret, as I
  have theirs:

That to myself (yes, I confess it privately, only to you, my beloved,
  my second self) I appear rather ugly.

Yes, spectacularly ugly.

What a relief to have that said, at last.

Yes, ugly. [ECHO: *Ugly!*] Hideous. [ECHO: *Hideous!*] Grotesque.
  [ECHO: *Grotesque!*]

What a pleasure to hear the truth spoken, for once in my life!

And in such a voice—so like my own—how impossibly lovely!

Swoons

DEPARTURES

(1973)

. . . and somewhere among the remote and vaulted ceilings of just such stations the farewells of the dead must long ago have left behind their still slowly diminishing echo.

One

ABC

A

A syllable with skin,
    tough and saurian,
    alive in the sewer's mouth.

A word with loot
    bulging its pockets,
    crouched in the alley after curfew.

A whole stanza forming
    to march off the curb
    and into your head with banners.

A poem in hiding
    from men in advertising
    and the guitars of ex-pilots.

B

Be the unfolding page,
    white page, memorial to the absolute,
    atlas of heights and depths,

Be the statue leaning out from the stone,
    the stone also, torn between past and future,
    and the hammer, whose strength we share.

C

See how the fearful chandelier
    trembles above you
    each time you open your mouth
    to sing. Sing.

Fragment: To a Mirror

Behind that bland facade of yours,
What drafts are moving down what intricate maze
Of halls? What solitude of attics waits,
Bleak, at the top of the still hidden stair?
And are those windows yours that open out
On such spectacular views?
Those still bays yours, where small boats lie
At anchor, abandoned by their crews?
The parks nearby,
Whose statues doze forever in the sun?
The stricken avenues,
Along which great palms wither and droop down
Their royal fronds,
And the parade is drummed
To a sudden inexplicable halt?
                              Tell me,
Is this the promised absence I foresee
In you, when no breath any more shall stir
The milky surface of the sleeping pond,
And you shall have back your rest at last,
Your half of nothingness?

A Letter

You write that you are ill, confused. The trees
Outside the window of the room they gave you
Are wet with tears each morning when they wake you
Out of the sleep you never quite fall into.
There is some dream of traffic in your head

That stops and goes, and goes, and does not stop
Sometimes all night, all day. The motorcade
Winds past you like the funeral cortege
Of someone famous you had slept with, once or twice.
(Another fit of tears dampens the leaves, the page.)

You would expose your wounds, pull down your blouse,
Unbosom yourself wholly to the young doctor
Who has the power to sign prescriptions, passes,
Who seems to like you . . . And so to pass
Into the city once again, one of us,

Hurrying by the damp trees of a park
Toward a familiar intersection where
The traffic signal warns you not to cross,
To wait, just as before, alone—but suddenly
Ten years older, tamed now, less mad, less beautiful.

A Dancer's Life

The lights in the theater fail. The long racks
Of costumes abandoned by the other dancers
Trouble Celeste. The conductor asks
If she is sad because autumn is coming on,

But when autumn comes she is merely pregnant and
    bored.
On her way back from the holidays, a man
Who appears to have no face rattles the door
To her compartment. *How disgusting,* she thinks;

How disgusting it always must be to grow old.
Dusk falls, and a few drops of rain.
On the train window trembles the blurred
Reflection of her own transparent beauty,

And through this, beautiful ruined cities passing,
Dark forests, and people everywhere
Pacing on lighted platforms, some
Beating their children, some apparently dancing.

The costumes of the dancers sway in the chill darkness.
Now sinking into sleep is like sinking again
Into the lake of her youth. Her parents
Lean from the rail of a ferryboat waving, waving,

As the boat glides farther out across the waves.
No one, it seems, is meeting her at the station.
The city is frozen. She warms herself
In the pink and scented twilight of a bar.

The waiter who serves her is young. She nods assent.
The conversation dies in bed. Later,
She hurries off to rehearsal. In the lobby,
Dizzy still with the weight of her own body,

She waits, surrounded by huge stills of herself
And bright posters announcing events to come.
Her life—she feels it closing about her now
Like a small theater, empty, without lights.

Portraits of the Sixties

1   PORTRAIT WITH SHORT HAIR

The days, the days!
And the scissors you cut
Your hair with—oh, how dull.
Time to change the needle.

Put on another record—
No, something baroque—
And think of the good times.
Think of lakes and rivers.

It's hot. Let in some air.
Let the smell of leftovers
Be one with the perfume
Of cooling asphalt, leaves.

And the nights? Ah, wonderful—
You alone,
Alone with the slums,
The flowerpots, the stars.

Think of the sea. Unzip,
Just as though someone were
Around to be made love to,
Or anyway to pose for.

The mysteries of sex!
Some day you'll wake up
Back on that Christmas morning
In Mexico, still a virgin.

What lonely aisles you prowled
In search of the forbidden,
Blinking your usher's torch,
Firefly of the balconies!

And when you found it—love!—
It was to pure French horns
Soaring above the plains
Of Saturday's Westerns.

The defiant eyes laughing
Into the sudden beam,
The soft Mexican curses,
The stains, the crushed corsages . . .

Poor spy, there's no disguise.
Your heart's as dark as
Theirs was and it speaks
With the same broken accent.

Those flowers, they blossom
Again now, tender buds
Of migraine—souvenirs.
And you call them poems,

Poems with hair slicked back,
Smelling of bay rum, sweat,
And hot buttered popcorn.
Furtive illuminations . . .

for Henri Coulette

3 PORTRAIT WITH TEQUILA

Pull down the shades.
Your black boyfriend is coming.
He's not like you. He wants
To live in the suburbs.

You want to paint. Your hand
Does your dreaming for you,
The same hand, braceleted with scars,
That smooths down cats, sheets, men.

Under it your body
Is turning into landscape—look!
Some metamorphosis
Of the moon . . . The ancients

Who watch you from their porches—
You in your earrings, in
Your bare feet, in that long
Boy's undershirt you wear

(Because your breasts are small)—
They're all asleep now,
The insects, the wind . . .
It's late. But then he's married,

And this is still Texas.
The night is a giant cactus.
Potent, aromatic,
The liquors you press from it.

They robbed you of your ticket
To the revolution, oh,
And then they stomped you good.
But nothing stops you.

You have identified yourself
To the police as quote
Lyric poet. What else?—
With fractured jaw. Orpheus,

Imperishable liar!
Your life's a poem still,
Broken iambs and all,
Jazz, jails—the complete works.

And one blue-silver line
Beyond the Antilles,
Vanishing . . . All fragments.
You who could scream across

The square in Cuernavaca,
At a friend you hadn't seen
For years, the one word, *bitch,*
And turn away—that's style!

Or this, your other voice,
This whisper along the wires
At night, like a dry wind,
Like conscience, always collect.

for Robert Boardman Vaughn

The newspaper on the table,
Confessing its lies.
The melon beside it,
Plump, unspoiled,

Trying to forget
That it was ever wrapped up
In anything so
Scandalous, so banal.

Already out, the knife,
Confident lover.
It smiles. It knows
How attractive it is

To sunlight. On the wall,
A guitar, in shadow,
Remembering hands . . .
I don't come into the picture.

Poets, O fellow exiles,
It's your scene now, and welcome.
You take up the guitar.
You cut up the melon.

But when are you going to
Roll up the newspaper, swat
The flies, take out all the garbage?
Mañana? Always mañana.

Lethargy

It smiles to see me
Still in my bathrobe.

It sits in my lap
And will not let me rise.

Now it is kissing my eyes.
Arms enfold me, arms

Pale with a thick down.
It seems I am falling asleep

To the sound of a story
Being read me.

This is the story.
Weeks have passed

Since first I lifted my hand
To set it down.

Luxury

You are like a sun of the tropics
Peering through blinds

Drawn for siesta.
Already you teach me

The Spanish for sunflower.
Such iridescence!

You, alone on the clean sheet,
Unadorned.

You, like the spilt moon.
You, like a star

Hidden by sun-goggles.
You shall have a thousand lovers.

You, spread here like butter,
Like doubloons, like flowers.

The Telephone Number of the Muse

Sleepily, the muse to me: "Let us be friends.
Good friends, but only friends. You understand."
And yawned. And kissed, for the last time, my ear.
Who earlier, weeping at my touch, had whispered:
"I loved you once." And: "No, I don't love him.
Not after everything he did." Later,
Rebuttoning her nightgown with my help:
"Sorry, I just have no desire, it seems."
Sighing: "For you, I mean." Long silence. Then:
"You always were so serious." At which
I smiled, darkly. And that was how I came
To sleep beside, not with her; without dreams.

I call her up sometimes, long distance now.
And she still knows my voice, but I can hear,
Beyond the music of her phonograph,
The laughter of the young men with their keys.

I have the number written down somewhere.

Twenty Questions

Is it raining out?
Is it raining in?
Are you a public fountain?
Are you an antique musical instrument?
Are you a famous resort, perhaps?
What is your occupation?
Are you by chance a body of water?
Do you often travel alone?
What is your native language, then?
Do you recall the word for carnation?

Are you sorry?
Will you be sorry?
Is this your handkerchief?
What is your destination?
Are you Aquarius?
Are you the watermelon flower?
Will you please take off your glasses?
Is this a holiday for you?
Is that a scar, or a birthmark?
Is there no word for calyx in your tongue?

On the Night of the Departure by Bus

Tell me if you were not happy in those days.
You were not yet twenty-five,
And you had not yet abandoned the guitar.

I swore to you by your nakedness that you were a guitar,
You swore to me by your nakedness that you were a guitar,
The moon swore to us both by your nakedness that you
      had abandoned yourself completely.

Who would not go on living?

The typewriter will be glad to have become the poem,
The guitar to have been your body,
I to have had the luck to envy the sole of your shoe in
      the dead of winter.

A passenger has lost his claim-check,
The brunette her barrette,
And I—I think that there are moths eating holes in my pockets,
That my place in line is evaporating,
That the moon is not the moon and the bus is not the bus.

What is the word for goodbye?

White Notes

1

Suddenly there was a dress,
Inhabited, in motion.

It contained a forest,
Small birds, rivers.

It contained the ivory
Of piano keys,
White notes.

Across the back of a chair
Skins of animals
Dried in the moon.

2

It happened.
Your body went out of your body.

It rose
To let the air in,
The night.

From the sheets it rose,
From the bare floor,
Floating.

Over roofs,
Smaller and smaller,
Lost.

Entangled now
In the cold arms
Of distant street lamps.

3

The city forgets where you live.
It wanders through many streets,
And the streets turn, confused,
Upon one another.

Parks have deserted themselves.
All night, awnings are whipped
And cannot remember.

O forgotten umbrella . . .
Darkness saw you, air
Displaced you, words
Erased you.

4

And afterwards,
After the quenching of the street lamps,
Long after the ivory could have been brought back to
    life by any touch.

Afterwards, when I might have told you
The address of your future.
Long after the future.

When the umbrella had been closed forever.
Then, when not even the moon
Would have the power to bruise you any more.

Then, in another time.

The Confession

You have no name, intimate crime;
There is nothing to whisper.
You have fled across many pillows,
But you leave nothing behind.

Dressed in the silence you were sworn to,
You passed without recognition.
No door holds you, no mirror;
I am the lone witness.

You have escaped into smoke,
Into the dark mouths of tunnels.
Once in the streets you were safe,
You were one among many.

The Success

He asks for directions, but the street
Is swaying before him drunkenly.
The buildings lean together. There is some
Conspiracy of drawn curtains against him.

And all around him he can sense the beauty
Of unseen arms, of eyes that slide off elsewhere.
Someone is living his life here, someone
Is turning back sheets meant to receive his body.

This is the address if not the destination.
The moonlight dies along his wrist. His hand
Slips off through the darkness on its stubborn mission,
Roving the row of mailboxes for the name it dreams.

He enters. The doorman vanishes with a nod.
The elevator ascends smoothly to his desire.
The light in the hall, the door against his cheek . . .
He has arrived. He recognizes the laughter.

The Assassination

It begins again, the nocturnal pulse.
It courses through the cables laid for it.
It mounts to the chandeliers and beats there, hotly.
We are too close. Too late, we would move back.
We are involved with the surge.

Now it bursts. Now it has been announced.
Now it is being soaked up by newspapers.
Now it is running through the streets.
The crowd has it. The woman selling carnations
And the man in the straw hat stand with it in their shoes.

Here is the red marquee it sheltered under,
Here is the ballroom, here
The sadly various orchestra led
By a single gesture. My arms open.
It enters. Look, we are dancing.

June 5, 1968

Two

America has so many roads—
On every road, someone lost.
And should we be sorry for the girls
Who will go into labor nine months from tonight?

Should we be sorry for being born
Americans? Here, lost at the crossroads,
Trying to find our place on the map.
So many towns, so many little stars . . .

America has surrounded us.
And the poems that fell from our mouths
Like stars in August—
Look for them in the Pacific.

after József

Lorcaesques

A song went looking for light
And met itself coming back.

*

The song with nothing to say
Has gone to sleep on my lips.

From a Notebook

1

Named ambassador
To the High Court of Prose,
I neglect my manners, my dress,
Speak in a loud voice, at length,
And am everywhere taken
For one of the natives.

2

Novelist and naturalist,
P. turns to poetry
In search, once more,
Of the true primitive.

May he locate the tribe,
Master the dialect.

3

Though, as G. says,
We American poets
No longer love words,
It is hard not to remember
What we felt for
Those that betrayed us,
Those we betrayed.

4

The Texas millionaire
Had offered to give the Church
Ten thousand dollars
In exchange for her virtue.

Advised by her priest
To follow her conscience,
She gave up
Working for charity.

5

AFTER THE CHINESE (I)

Near the summit,
They rest on separate rocks, smoking,
And wonder whether the wildflowers
Are worth going on for.

6

After the overture,
The opera seemed brief.

7

FROM A SPY NOVEL: "Maybe you knew Bliss by another name."

8

WORKSHOP

G. maintains that the Adjective somehow penetrates
the Noun with all that is most private, thereby becoming
the most Personal of the Parts of Speech, hence the
most Beautiful.

I, on the contrary, maintain that the Conjunction, being Impersonal, is the more Beautiful, and especially when suppressed.

9

M., opening my diary, found the pages blank.

10

AFTER THE CHINESE (II)

Discs for a cough,
A smooth stone for remembrance.

And the man in the old song,
For a single quince out of season,
Sent back a poem that lasted
Three thousand years.

Riddle

White of a blind man's eye
I saw rolling.
When the lid closed over,
Dark was twice dark.

Soon I saw glitter
His other eye.
Dew fell then; dark scattered.
What it saw, men saw.

(THE MOON AND THE SUN)

for Stephen Dobyns

Things

Hard, but you can polish it.
Precious, it has eyes. Can wound.
Would dance upon water. Sinks.
Stays put. Crushed, becomes a road.

(STONE)

Mine to give, mine to offer
No resistance. Mine
To receive you, mine to keep
The shape of our nights.

(PILLOW)

My former friend, my traitor.
My too easily broken.
My still to be escaped from.

(MIRROR)

To support this roof.
To stand up. To take
Such weight in the knees . . .
To keep the secret.
To envy no cloud.

(WALL)

Three

An Elegy Is Preparing Itself

There are pines that are tall enough
Already. In the distance,
The whining of saws; and needles,
Silently slipping through the chosen cloth.
The stone, then as now, unfelt,
Perfectly weightless. And certain words,
That will come together to mourn,
Waiting, in their dark clothes, apart.

Variations on a Text by Vallejo

Me moriré en París con aguacero . . .

I will die in Miami in the sun,
On a day when the sun is very bright,
A day like the days I remember, a day like other days,
A day that nobody knows or remembers yet,
And the sun will be bright then on the dark glasses of strangers
And in the eyes of a few friends from my childhood
And of the surviving cousins by the graveside,
While the diggers, standing apart, in the still shade of the palms,
Rest on their shovels, and smoke,
Speaking in Spanish softly, out of respect.

I think it will be on a Sunday like today,
Except that the sun will be out, the rain will have stopped,
And the wind that today made all the little shrubs kneel down;
And I think it will be a Sunday because today,
When I took out this paper and began to write,
Never before had anything looked so blank,
My life, these words, the paper, the gray Sunday;
And my dog, quivering under a table because of the storm,
Looked up at me, not understanding,
And my son read on without speaking, and my wife slept.

Donald Justice is dead. One Sunday the sun came out,
It shone on the bay, it shone on the white buildings,
The cars moved down the street slowly as always, so many,
Some with their headlights on in spite of the sun,
And after a while the diggers with their shovels

Walked back to the graveside through the sunlight,
And one of them put his blade into the earth
To lift a few clods of dirt, the black marl of Miami,
And scattered the dirt, and spat,
Turning away abruptly, out of respect.

Poem

This poem is not addressed to you.
You may come into it briefly,
But no one will find you here, no one.
You will have changed before the poem will.

Even while you sit there, unmovable,
You have begun to vanish. And it does not matter.
The poem will go on without you.
It has the spurious glamor of certain voids.

It is not sad, really, only empty.
Once perhaps it was sad, no one knows why.
It prefers to remember nothing.
Nostalgias were peeled from it long ago.

Your type of beauty has no place here.
Night is the sky over this poem.
It is too black for stars.
And do not look for any illumination.

You neither can nor should understand what it means.
Listen, it comes without guitar,
Neither in rags nor any purple fashion.
And there is nothing in it to comfort you.

Close your eyes, yawn. It will be over soon.
You will forget the poem, but not before
It has forgotten you. And it does not matter.
It has been most beautiful in its erasures.

O bleached mirrors! Oceans of the drowned!
Nor is one silence equal to another.
And it does not matter what you think.
This poem is not addressed to you.

Homage to the Memory of Wallace Stevens

Hartford is cold today but no colder for your absence.
The rain is green over Avon and, since your death, the sky
Has been blue many times with a blue you did not imagine.

The judges of Key West sit soberly in black
But only because it is their accustomed garb,
And the sea sings with the same voice still, neither serious nor
    sorry.

The walls past which you walked in your white suit,
Ponderous, pondering French pictures,
Are no less vivid now. Not one is turned to the wall.

The actuarial tables are not upset.
The mail travels back and forth to Ceylon as before.
The gold leaf peels in season and is renewed.

And there are heroes who falter but do not fall,
Or fall without faltering and without fault,
But you were not one of them. Nevertheless,

The poet practicing his scales
Thinks of you as his thumbs slip clumsily under and under,
Avoiding the darker notes.

2

The *the* has become an *a*. The dictionary
Closed at dusk, along with the zoo in the park,

And the wings of the swans are folded now like the sheets
     of a long letter.
Who borrows your French words and postures now?

3

The opera of the gods is finished,
And the applause is dying.
The chorus will soon be coming down from the clouds.
Even their silence may be understood
As a final platitude of sorts, a summing up.

The tireless dancers have retired at last
To a small apartment on a treeless street.
But, oh, the pas de deux of Eden begins again
On cotsprings creaking like the sun and moon!
The operation of the universe is temporarily suspended.

What has been good? What has been beautiful?
The tuning up, or the being put away?
The instruments have nothing more to say.
Now they will sleep on plush and velvet till
Our breath revives them to new flutterings, new adieux—

And to the picnic all the singers come,
Minus their golden costumes, but no less gods for that.
Now all quotations from the text apply,
Including the laughter, including the offstage thunder,
Including even this almost human cry.

Sonatina in Green

One spits on the sublime.
One lies in bed alone, reading
Yesterday's newspaper. One
Has composed a beginning, say,
A phrase or two. No more!
There has been traffic enough
In the boudoir of the muse.

And still they come, demanding entrance,
Noisy, and with ecstatic cries
Catching the perfume, forcing their way—
For them, what music? Only,
Distantly, through some door ajar,
Echoes, broken strains; and the garland
Crushed at the threshold.

                    And we,
We few with the old instruments,
Obstinate, sounding the one string—
For us, what music? Only, at times,
The sunlight of late afternoon
That plays in the corner of a room,
Playing upon worn keys. At times,
Smells of decaying greenery, faint bouquets—
More than enough.

And our cries
Diminish behind us:
                              Cover
The bird cages! No more
Bargain days in the flower stalls!
There has been traffic enough
In the boudoir of the muse,
More than enough traffic.
                              Or say
That one composed, in the end,
Another beginning, in spite of all this,
Sublime. Enough!

Closed are the grand boulevards,
And closed those mouths that made the lesser songs,
And the curtains drawn in the boudoir.

for my students

Sonatina in Yellow

Du schnell vergehendes Daguerreotyp
in meinen langsamer vergehenden Händen.
— RILKE

The pages of the album,
As they are turned, turn yellow; a word,
Once spoken, obsolete,
No longer what was meant. Say it.
The meanings come, or come back later,
Unobtrusive, taking their places.

Think of the past. Think of forgetting the past.
It was an exercise requiring further practice;
A difficult exercise, played through by someone else.
Overheard from another room now
It seems full of mistakes.
                        So the voice of your father,
Rising as from the next room still
With all the remote but true affection of the dead,
Repeats itself, insists,
Insisting you must listen, rises
In the familiar pattern of reproof
For some childish error, a nap disturbed,
Or vase, broken or overturned;
Rises and subsides. And you do listen.
Listen and forget. Practice forgetting.

Forgotten sunlight still
Blinds the eyes of faces in the album.
The faces fade, and there is only
A sort of meaning that comes back,
Or for the first time comes, but comes too late
To take the places of the faces.

                    Remember
The dead air of summer. Remember
The trees drawn up to their full height like fathers,
The underworld of shade you entered at their feet.
Enter the next room. Enter it quietly now,
Not to disturb your father sleeping there. *He stirs.*
Notice his clothes, how scrupulously clean,
Unwrinkled from the nap; his face, freckled with work,
Smoothed by a passing dream. The vase
Is not yet broken, the still young roses
Drink there from perpetual waters. *He rises, speaks . . .*

Repeat it now, no one was listening.
So your hand moves, moving across the keys,
And slowly the keys grow darker to the touch.

Three Odes

COOL DARK ODE

You could have sneaked up,
Broken into those overheated rooms
By the windows overlooking the tavern,
Or the back way, by the broad but unlighted stairs,
When the long planed table that served as a desk
Was recalling the quiet of the woods,
When the books, older, were thinking farther back
To the same essential stillness,
And both table and books, if they thought of the future ever,
Probably shuddered, as though from a stray draft,
Seeing themselves as eventual flame,
Some final smoke.

Now, when there is no longer any occasion,
I think of inviting you in
To wait for us
On the short, cramped sofa,
Beside the single candle stub
Which must have frightened you off then,
Or in the cubicle of the bedroom,
Where even then we imagined ourselves extinguished
By your total embrace,
Attentive meanwhile to the animal noises of your breathing,
The whimpers,
The sudden intoxicated outcries,
That were not our own.

Night, night, O blackness of winter,
I tell you this, you
That used to come up as far as the frosted panes, the door,
As far as the edges of our skin,
Without any thought, I know now,
Of entering those borrowed rooms,
Or even our mouths, our eyes,
Which all too often were carelessly left open for you.

It was still possible then
To imagine that no more than one or two hands
Would ever move down the face of the hour,
And that the shadow which followed
Might remain patient
And, if anything, somewhat reluctant to continue;
That no more than one or two hands
Had ever descended so far
As the shoulders of the afternoon,
And that, necessarily, they would have been bare then
Of even that shadow which, sometimes, the air itself
    seems to be charged with
And to suffer from;
That no more than one or two hands surely
Would have crossed the forbidden zone
At the end of summer,
And that the sky there would be turning always from
    white to pink, slowly,
And that it could no longer matter then
What shadows rose from your hollows and sank back.

And it is still possible to imagine
That there are one or two hands
Which do not know, or which do not yet know,
Anything of either that face or the shadow
Which does, after all, follow,
Or of flushed shoulders or turning sky,
Or of those particular hollows, alive
With less and less curious and impulsive shadows now;
And that there may somewhere be hands
Which will never be smeared with the very special pollen
And general muskiness of a dying summer;
And that there are probably other hands which have stopped,
Or will stop, or even now are shaken with premonitions
Of a time when they will have begun to stop,

And among these some which remember little or nothing
Of you and your coloring,
And some also which do not and cannot forget
Your blood upon them and your dew.

PALE TEPID ODE

Not with the vague smoke
In the curtains,
Not with the pigeons or doves
Under the eaves,
Nevertheless you are there, hidden,
And again you wake me,
Scentless, noiseless,
Someone or something,
Something or someone faithless,
And that will not return.

Undiscovered star,
That fade and are fading,
But never entirely fading,
Fixed,
And that will not return.

Someone, someone or something,
Colorless, formless,
And that will not return.

Absences

It's snowing this afternoon and there are no flowers.
There is only this sound of falling, quiet and remote,
Like the memory of scales descending the white keys
Of a childhood piano—outside the window, palms!
And the heavy head of the cereus, inclining,
Soon to let down its white or yellow-white.

Now, only these poor snow-flowers in a heap,
Like the memory of a white dress cast down . . .
So much has fallen.
            And I, who have listened for a step
All afternoon, hear it now, but already falling away,
Already in memory. And the terrible scales descending
On the silent piano; the snow; and the absent flowers
    abounding.

Presences

Everyone, everyone went away today.
They left without a word, and I think
I did not hear a single goodbye today.

And all that I saw was someone's hand, I think,
Thrown up out there like the hand of someone drowning,
But far away, too far to be sure what it was or meant.

No, but I saw how everything had changed
Later, just as the light had; and at night
I saw that from dream to dream everything changed.

And those who might have come to me in the night,
The ones who did come back but without a word,
All those I remembered passed through my hands like clouds—

Clouds out of the south, familiar clouds—
But I could not hold on to them, they were drifting away,
Everything going away in the night again and again.

From SELECTED POEMS

(*1979*)

Little Elegy → This Is on Elegy

Weep, all you girls
Who prize good looks and song.
Mack, the canary, is dead.

Death comes to all, & hurts those around it.

A girl very much like you
Kept him by her twelve months
Close as a little brother.

He perched where he pleased,
Hopped, chirping, from breast to breast,
And fed, sometimes, pecking from her mouth.

where the heart is, life where breath came from, life

onomatopia

O lucky bird! But death
Plucks from the air even
The swiftest, the most favored.

moreso, cause birds fly in the air

Red are the eyes of his mistress now.
On us, her remaining admirers,
They do not yet quite focus.

She cant think of anything yet, but the bird

death takes everyone

after Catullus

177

First Death

JUNE 12, 1933

I saw my grandmother grow weak.
When she died, I kissed her cheek.

I remember the new taste—
Powder mixed with a drying paste.

*of death
Child will
associate
w/ death*

Down the hallway, on its table,
Lay the family's great Bible.

In the dark, by lamplight stirred,
The Void grew pregnant with the Word.

In black ink they wrote it down.
The older ink was turning brown.

From the woods there came a cry,
The hoot owl asking who not why.

*what he/she
wants to
know*

Calculating, unfeeling

The men sat silent on the porch,
Each lighted pipe a friendly torch

*helping
each other
through it*

Against the unknown and the known.
But the child knew himself alone.

*her/his first
to their many,
different
to him.*

178

JUNE 13, 1933

The morning sun rose up and stuck.
Sunflower strove with hollyhock.

I ran the worn path past the sty.
Nothing was hidden from God's eye.

The barn door creaked. I walked among
Chaff and wrinkled cakes of dung.

In the dim light I read the dates
On the dusty license plates

Nailed to the wall as souvenirs.
I breathed the dust in of the years.

I circled the abandoned Ford
Before I tried the running board.

At the wheel I felt the heat
Press upward through the springless seat.

And when I touched the silent horn,
Small mice scattered through the corn.

June 14, 1933

I remember the soprano
Fanning herself at the piano,

And the preacher looming large
Above me in his dark blue serge.

My shoes brought in a smell of clay
To mingle with the faint sachet

Of flowers sweating in their vases.
A stranger showed us to our places.

The stiff fan stirred in mother's hand.
Air moved, but only when she fanned.

I wondered how could all her grief
Be squeezed into one small handkerchief.

There was a buzzing on the sill.
It stopped, and everything was still.

We bowed our heads, we closed our eyes
To the mercy of the flies.

Two Blues

1   THE SOMETIME DANCER BLUES

When the lights go on uptown,
Why do you feel so low, honey,
Why do you feel so low-down?

When the piano and the trombone start,
Why do you feel so blue, honey,
Like a rubber glove had reached in for your heart?

Oh, when the dancers take the floor,
Why don't you step out with them, honey,
Why won't you step out with them any more?

The stars are gone and the night is dark,
Except for the radium, honey,
That glows on the hands of the bedside clock,

The little hands that go around and around,
Oh, as silently as time, honey,
Without a sound, without a sound.

A dark time is coming, and the gypsy knows what else.
Fly away, O angel death.

It looks like a raven sitting on the wire.
It looks like a raven sitting on the telephone wire.
Oh, it is some high flyer!

Look out now, it's got loose in the yard.
Look out, look out, it's loose in the back yard.
Oh, no, don't you look at me, big bird.

If you are lost, I can't help.
If you are lost, I can't help.
I am a stranger in this place myself.

Fly away, fly away,
Fly away, O angel death.

And shine down, moonlight, make those long feathers
      shine.
I want to keep track of where it's going.
[*Spoken*] Shine down, moonlight.

Unflushed Urinals

lines written in the Omaha bus station

Seeing them, I recognize the contempt
Some men have for themselves.

This man, for instance, zipping quickly up, head turned,
Like a bystander innocent of his own piss.

And here comes one to repair himself at the mirror,
Patting down damp, sparse hairs, suspiciously still black,
Poor bantam cock of a man, jaunty at one a.m., perfumed,
    undiscourageable . . .

O the saintly forbearance of these mirrors!
The acceptingness of the washbowls, in which we absolve
    ourselves!

Sunday Afternoon in Buffalo, Texas

bus stop, 4:30 p.m.

Four or five roads converge here, going somewhere else.

And on the concrete apron of the Conoco station
This boy all afternoon has practiced squealing his new radials
With the sound of a young giantess repeatedly climaxing.

One carload of the converted, dressed for evening service,
Parks on thin grass beside the highway—nothing to do
But watch us stumble, thirsty and disheveled, down the bus steps.

The Buffalo Flower Shop is closed; on its door
The little paper clock is set for tomorrow. But I
Will dream tonight of the wild buffalo flower, O rare and shaggy!

Leaving town, we pass a yard made colorful
By red and yellow flowerpots strung between trees,
Like lanterns left on after some long and marvelous party.

Population: One-Two-Four-Two . . .

Memories of the Depression Years

1   A FARM NEAR TIFTON, GEORGIA, C. 1930

. . . in the kitchen, as she bends to serve,
Aunt Babe's too finely thin, upgathered hair
Filters the sunlight coming through behind
(Which is how Griffith lights his heroines).
Moth wings cling to the door screen; dust motes whirl.
There is such a light!
                              The grown-ups chatter on,
Unheard. Meanwhile I listen for the freight,
Due any minute. I can *see* the bell
Swing back and forth in close-up, silently,
The huge wheels revolving, the steam rising . . .
But already the silent world is lost forever.

2   BOSTON, GEORGIA, C. 1933

The tin roofs catch the slanting sunlight.
A few cows turn homeward up back lanes;
Boys with sticks nudge the cattle along.
A pickup whines past. The dust rises.
Crows call. Cane sweetens along the stalk.
All around, soundlessly, gnats hover.
And from his stoop now my grandfather
Stands watching as all this comes to pass.

3   MIAMI, FLORIDA, C. 1936

Our new house on the edge of town
Looks bare at first, and raw. A pink
Plaster flamingo on one leg
Stands preening by the lily pond.
And just as the sun begins to sink
Into the Everglades beyond,
It seems to shatter against the pane
In little asterisks of light,
And on our lids half-closed in prayer
Over the clean blue willowware.

In the Attic

There's a half hour toward dusk when flies,
Trapped by the summer screens, expire
Musically in the dust of sills;
And ceilings slope toward remembrance.

The same crimson afternoons expire
Over the same few rooftops repeatedly;
Only, being stored up for remembrance,
They somehow escape the ordinary.

Childhood is like that, repeatedly
Lost in the very longueurs it redeems.
One forgets how small and ordinary
The world looked once by dusklight from above . . .

But not the moment which redeems
The drowsy arias of the flies—
And the chin settles onto palms above
Numbed elbows propped on rotting sills.

Thinking About the Past

Certain moments will never change nor stop being—
My mother's face all smiles, all wrinkles soon;
The rock wall building, built, collapsed then, fallen;
Our upright loosening downward slowly out of tune—
All fixed into place now, all rhyming with each other.
That red-haired girl with wide mouth—Eleanor—
Forgotten thirty years—her freckled shoulders, hands.
The breast of Mary Something, freed from a white swimsuit,
Damp, sandy, warm; or Margery's, a small, caught bird—
Darkness they rise from, darkness they sink back toward.
O marvelous early cigarettes! O bitter smoke, Benton!
And Kenny in wartime whites, crisp, cocky,
Time a bow bent with his certain failure.
Dusks, dawns; waves; the ends of songs . . .

Childhood

J'ai heurté, savez-vous, d'incroyables Florides . . .
—RIMBAUD

TIME: *the thirties*
PLACE: *Miami, Florida*

Once more beneath my thumb the globe turns—
And doomed republics pass in a blur of colors . . .

         Winter mornings now my grandfather,
Head bared to the mild sunshine, likes to spread
The Katzenjammers out around a white lawn chair
To catch the stray curls of citrus from his knife.
Chameleons quiver in ambush; wings
Of monarchs beat above bronze turds, feasting.
        And there are pilgrim ants
Eternally bearing incommensurate crumbs
Past slippered feet. There,
In the lily pond, my own face wrinkles
With the slow teasings of a stick.
        The long days pass, days
Streaked with the colors of the first embarrassments.
And Sundays, among kin, happily ignored,
I sit nodding, somnolent with horizons.
        Myriad tiny suns
Drown in the deep mahogany polish of the chair arms;
Bunched cushions prickle through starched cotton . . .

        Already
I know the pleasure of certain solitudes.
I can look up at a ceiling so theatrical
Its stars seem more aloof than the real stars;
And pre-depression putti blush in the soft glow

Of exit signs. Often I blink, reentering
The world—or catch, surprised, in a shop window,
My ghostly image skimming across nude mannequins.
Drawbridges, careless of traffic, lean there
Against the low clouds—early evening . . .

All day

There is a smell of ocean longing landward.
And, high on his frail ladder, my father
Stands hammering great storm shutters down
Across the windows of the tall hotels,
Swaying. Around downed wires, across broken fronds,
Our Essex steers, barge-like and slow.

Westward now

The smoky rose of oblivion blooms, hangs;
And on my knee a small red sun-glow, setting.
For a long time I feel, coming and going in waves,
The stupid wish to cry. I dream . . .

And there are

Colognes that mingle on the barber's hands
Swathing me in his striped cloth, Saturdays, downtown.
Billy, the midget haberdasher, stands grinning
Under the winking neon goat, his sign,
As Flagler's sidewalks fill. Slowly
The wooden escalator rattles upward
Toward the twin fountains of the mezzanine
Where boys, secretly brave, prepare to taste
The otherness trickling there, forbidden . . .

And then the warm cashews in cool arcades!

O counters of spectacles!—where the bored child first
Scans new perspectives squinting through strange lenses;
And the mirrors, tilting, offer back toy sails
Stiffening breezeless toward green shores of baize . . .

How thin the grass looks of the new yards—
                    And everywhere
The fine sand burning into the bare heels
With which I learn to crush, going home,
The giant sandspurs of the vacant lots.
Iridescences of mosquito hawks
Glimmer above brief puddles filled with skies,
Tropical and changeless. And sometimes,
Where the city halts, the cracked sidewalks
Lead to a coral archway still spanning
The entrance to some wilderness of palmetto—

Forlorn suburbs, but with golden names!

dedicated to the poets of a mythical childhood:
Wordsworth, Rimbaud, Rilke, Hart Crane, Alberti

THE SUNSET MAKER

(*1987*)

Lines at the New Year

    1

The old year slips past
          unseen, the way a snake goes.
Vanishes,
          and the grass closes behind it.

    2

No clouds—and the grayblues
          subside into saffron.
Delicately they subside,
          into the saffron.

Mule Team and Poster

Two mules stand waiting in front of the brick wall of a warehouse,
      hitched to a shabby flatbed wagon.
Its spoked wheels resemble crude wooden flowers
      pulled recently from a deep and stubborn mud.

The rains have passed over for now
      and the sun is back,
Invisible, but everywhere present,
      and of a special brightness, like God.

The way the poster for the traveling show
      still clings to its section of the wall,
It looks as though a huge door stood open
      or a terrible flap of brain had been peeled back, revealing

Someone's idea of heaven:
      seven dancing-girls, caught on the upkick,
All in fringed dresses and bobbed hair.
      One wears a Spanish comb and has an escort . . .

Meanwhile the mules crunch patiently the few cornshucks
      someone has thoughtfully scattered for them.
The poster is torn in places, slightly crumpled;
      a few bricks, here and there, show through.

And a long shadow—
      the last shade perhaps in all of Alabama—
Stretches beneath the wagon, crookedly,
      like a great scythe laid down there and forgotten.

on a photograph by Walker Evans (Alabama, 1936)

My South

I dont! I dont hate it! I dont hate it!

— Q. COMPSON

But why do I write of the all unutterable and the all abysmal? Why does my pen not drop from my hand on approaching the infinite pity and tragedy of all the past? It does, poor helpless pen, with what it meets of the ineffable, what it meets of the cold Medusa-face of life, of all the life lived, on every side. Basta, basta!

— H. JAMES

1 ON THE PORCH

There used to be a way the sunlight caught
The cocoons of caterpillars in the pecans.
A boy's shadow would lengthen to a man's
Across the yard then, slowly. And if you thought
Some sleepy god had dreamed it all up—well,
There stood my grandfather, Lincoln-tall and solemn,
Tapping his pipe out on a white-flaked column,
Carefully, carefully, as though it were his job.
(And we would watch the pipe-stars as they fell.)
As for the quiet, the same train always broke it.
Then the great silver watch rose from his pocket
For us to check the hour, the dark fob
Dangling the watch between us like a moon.
It would be evening soon then, very soon.

2   At the Cemetery

Above the fence-flowers, like a bloody thumb,
A hummingbird is throbbing. . . . And some
Petals take motion from the beaten wings
In hardly observable obscure quiverings.
My mother stands there, but so still her clothing
Seems to have settled into stone, nothing
To animate her face, nothing to read there—
O plastic rose O clouds O still cedar!
She stands this way for a long time while the sky
Ponders her with its great Medusa-eye;
Or in my memory she does. And then a
Slow blacksnake, lazy with long sunning, slides
Down from its slab, and through the thick grass, and hides
Somewhere among the purpling wild verbena.

3   On the Farm

And I, missing the city intensely at that moment,
Moped and sulked at the window. I heard the first owl, quite near,
But the sound hardly registered. And the kerosene lamp
Went on sputtering, giving off vague medicinal fumes
That made me think of sickrooms. I had been memorizing
"The Ballad of Reading Gaol," but the lamplight hurt my eyes;
And I was too bored to sleep, restless and bored.
                                                  Years later,
Perhaps, I will recall the evenings, empty and vast, when
Under the first stars, there by the back gate, secretly, I
Would relieve myself on the shamed and drooping hollyhocks.
Now I yawned; the old dream of being a changeling returned.
The owl cried, and I felt myself like the owl—alone, proud,
Almost invisible—or like some hero in Homer
Protected by a cloud let down by the gods to save him.

4   On the Train, Heading North Through
     Florida, Late at Night and Long Ago, and
     Ending with a Line from Thomas Wolfe

Midnight or after, and the little lights
Glitter like lost beads from a broken necklace
Beyond smudged windows, lost and irretrievable—
Some promise of romance these Southern nights
Never entirely keep—unless, sleepless,
We should pass down dim corridors again
To stand, braced in a swaying vestibule,
Alone with the darkness and the wind—out there
Nothing but pines and one new road perhaps,
Straight and white, aimed at the distant gulf—
And hear, from the smoking room, the sudden high-pitched
Whinny of laughter pass from throat to throat;
And the great wheels smash and pound beneath our feet.

American Scenes (1904–1905)

1 CAMBRIDGE IN WINTER

Immense pale houses! Sunshine just now and snow
Light up and pauperize the whole brave show—
Each fanlight, each veranda, each good address,
All a mere paint and pasteboard paltriness!

These winter sunsets are the one fine thing:
Blood on the snow, some last impassioned fling,
The wild frankness and sadness of surrender—
As if our cities ever could be tender!

2 RAILWAY JUNCTION SOUTH OF RICHMOND, PAST MIDNIGHT

Indistinguishable engines hooting, red
Fires flaring, vanishing; a formless shed
Just straggling lifeward before sinking back
Into Dantean glooms beside the track,

All steam and smoke and earth—and even here,
Out of this little hell of spurts and hisses,
Come the first waftings of the Southern air,
Of open gates, of all but bland abysses.

3   St. Michael's Cemetery, Charleston

One may depend on these old cemeteries
To say the one charmed thing there is to say—
So here the silvery seaward outlook carries
Hints of some other world beyond the bay,

The sun-warmed tombs, the flowers. Each faraway
Game-haunted inlet and reed-smothered isle
Speaks of lost Venices; and the South meanwhile
Has only to be tragic to beguile.

4   Epilogue: Coronado Beach, California

In a hotel room by the sea, the Master
Sits brooding on the continent he has crossed.
Not that he foresees immediate disaster,
Only a sort of freshness being lost—
Or should he go on calling it Innocence?
The sad-faced monsters of the plains are gone;
Wall Street controls the wilderness. There's an immense
Novel in all this waiting to be done,
But not, not—sadly enough   by him. His talents,
Such as they may be, want an older theme,
One rather more civilized than this, on balance.
For him now always the consoling dream
Is just the mild dear light of Lamb House falling
Beautifully down the pages of his calling.

after Henry James

Nineteenth-Century Portrait

Under skies God Himself must have painted blue
You came with your basket from the marketplace,
Bananas and a few ripe pineapples in it for the Boss.

Your skirt, all scarlet, and swinging with each step,
Was like the bright cape matadors show the bull;
The same cloth wound about your forehead, a richly bled bandage.

The morning of the world sat in its palm branch,
A just-escaped parrot. Big mosquitoes hummed.
White men smoked on their verandas, each safe in his own small
        cloud.

I can imagine the straw mat you woke from;
Your dreams, too, all hummingbirds and hibiscus;
And everything I imagine is like you, simple and fresh.

I think you must have wanted to see the States,
And even then our cities were too crowded.
Down by the docks, in winter, the cold fogs could not have hidden

The truth from you very long. Fate was the rags
You stood shivering in, under the lampposts,
Above which must have risen, sometimes, tall ghosts of absent
        palms.

after Baudelaire

202

Young Girls Growing Up (*1911*)

No longer do they part and scatter so hopelessly before you,
But they will stop and put an elbow casually
On the piano top and look quite frankly at you,
Their pale reflections gliding there like swans.

What you say to them now is not lost. They listen to the end
And—little heart-shaped chins uplifted—seem
Just on the point of breaking into song;
Nor is a short conversation more than they can stand.

When they turn away now they do so slowly, and mean no harm;
And it seems their backs are suddenly broader also.
You picture yourself in the avenue below, masked by trees,
And, just as the street lamps go on, you glance up:

There, there at the window, blotting out the light . . . !
Weeks pass and perhaps you meet unexpectedly,
And now they come forward mournfully, hands outstretched,
Asking why you are such a stranger, what has changed?

But when you seek them out, they only
Crouch in a window seat and pretend to read,
And have no look to spare you, and seem cruel.
And this is why there are men who wander aimlessly through
    cities!

This is why there are cities, and darkness, and a river;
And men who stride along the embankment now, without a plan,
And turn their collars up against the moon,
Saying to one another: *Live, we must try to live, my friend!*

after Kafka

Children Walking Home from School
Through Good Neighborhood

They are like figures held in some glass ball,
One of those in which, when shaken, snowstorms occur;
But this one is not yet shaken.
            And they go unaccompanied still,
Out along this walkway between two worlds,
This almost swaying bridge.
            October sunlight checkers their path;
It frets their cheeks and bare arms now with shadow
Almost too pure to signify itself.
And they progress slowly, somewhat lingeringly,
Independent, yet moving all together,
Like polyphonic voices that crisscross
In short-lived harmonies.

            Today, a few stragglers.
One, a girl, stands there with hands spaced out, so—
A gesture in a story. Someone's school notebook spills,
And they bend down to gather up the loose pages.
(Bright sweaters knotted at the waist; solemn expressions.)
Not that they would shrink or hold back from what may come,
For now they all at once run to meet it, a little swirl of colors,
Like the leaves already blazing and falling farther north.

October: A Song

Summer, goodbye.
The days grow shorter.
Cranes walk the fairway now
In careless order.

They step so gradually
Toward the distant green
They might almost be brushstrokes
Animating a screen.

Mists canopy
The water hazard.
Nearby, a little flag
Lifts, brave but frazzled.

Under sad clouds
Two white-capped golfers
Stand looking off, dreamy and strange,
Like young girls in Balthus.

Sea Wind: A Song

Sea wind, you rise
From the night waves below,
Not that we see you come and go,
But as the blind know things we know
And feel you on our face,
And all you are
Or ever were is space,
Sea wind, come from so far
To fill us with this restlessness
That will outlast your own—
So the fig tree,
When you are gone,
Sea wind, still bends and leans out toward the sea
And goes on blossoming alone.

after Rilke

Last Evening: At the Piano

And night and far to go—
For hours the convoys had rolled by
Like storm clouds in a troubled sky;
   He'd gone on playing, though,

And raised his eyes to hers,
Which had become his mirror now,
So filled were they with his clenched brow,
   And the pain to come, or worse;

And then the image blurred.
She stood at the window in the gloom
And looked back through the fading room—
   Outside, a fresh wind stirred—

And noticed across a chair
The officer's jacket he had flung
There earlier; and now it hung
   Like the coats scarecrows wear

And which the bird-shadows flee and scatter from;
Or like the skin of some great battle drum.

after Rilke

Psalm and Lament

Hialeah, Florida
in memory of my mother (1897–1971)

The clocks are sorry, the clocks are very sad.
One stops, one goes on striking the wrong hours.

And the grass burns terribly in the sun,
The grass turns yellow secretly at the roots.

Now suddenly the yard chairs look empty, the sky looks empty,
The sky looks vast and empty.

Out on Red Road the traffic continues; everything continues.
Nor does memory sleep; it goes on.

Out spring the butterflies of recollection,
And I think that for the first time I understand

The beautiful ordinary light of this patio
And even perhaps the dark rich earth of a heart.

(The bedclothes, they say, had been pulled down.
I will not describe it. I do not want to describe it.

No, but the sheets were drenched and twisted.
They were the very handkerchiefs of grief.)

Let summer come now with its schoolboy trumpets and fountains.
But the years are gone, the years are finally over.

And there is only
This long desolation of flower-bordered sidewalks

That runs to the corner, turns, and goes on,
That disappears and goes on

Into the black oblivion of a neighborhood and a world
Without billboards or yesterdays.

Sometimes a sad moon comes and waters the roof tiles.
But the years are gone. There are no more years.

In Memory of My Friend, the Bassoonist, John Lenox

Coconut Grove

1

One winter he was the best
Contrabassoonist south
Of Washington, D.C.—
The only one. Lonely

In eminence he sat,
Like some lost island king,
High on a second-story porch
Overlooking the bay

(His blue front lawn, his kingdom)
And presided over the Shakespearean
Feuds and passions of the eave-pigeons.
Who, during the missile crisis,

Had stocked his boat with booze,
Charts, and the silver flute
He taught himself to play,
Casually, one evening.

And taught himself to see,
Sailing thick glasses out blindly
Over some lily-choked canal.
O autodidact supreme!

2

John, where you are now can you see?
Do the pigeons there bicker like ours?
Does the deep bassoon not moan
Or the flute sigh ever?

No one could think it was you,
Slumped there on the sofa, despairing,
The hideous green sofa.
No, you are off somewhere,

Off with Gauguin and Christian
Amid hibiscus'd isles,
Red-mustached, pink-bearded
Again, as in early manhood.

It is well. Shark waters
Never did faze you half so much
As the terrible radios
And booboiseries of the neighbors.

Here, if you care, the bay
Is printed with many boats now,
Thick as trash; that high porch is gone,
Gone up in the smoke of money, money;

The barbarians . . .
                        But enough.
You are missed. Across the way,
Someone is practicing sonatas,
And the sea air smells again of good gin.

In Memory of the Unknown Poet, Robert Boardman Vaughn

> *But the essential advantage for a poet is not, to have a beautiful world with which to deal: it is to be able to see beneath both beauty and ugliness; to see the boredom, and the horror, and the glory.*
>
> —T. S. ELIOT

It was his story. It would always be his story.
It followed him; it overtook him finally—
The boredom, and the horror, and the glory.

Probably at the end he was not yet sorry,
Even as the boots were brutalizing him in the alley.
It was his story. It would always be his story.

Blown on a blue horn, full of sound and fury,
But signifying, O signifying magnificently
The boredom, and the horror, and the glory.

I picture the snow as falling without hurry
To cover the cobbles and the toppled ashcans completely.
It was his story. It would always be his story.

Lately he had wandered between St. Mark's Place and the Bowery,
Already half a spirit, mumbling and muttering sadly.
O the boredom, and the horror, and the glory.

All done now. But I remember the fiery
Hypnotic eye and the raised voice blazing with poetry.
It was his story and would always be his story—
The boredom, and the horror, and the glory.

Hell

R. B. Vaughn speaks:

"After so many years of pursuing the ideal
I came home. But I had caught sight of it.
You see it sometimes in the blue-silver wake
Of island schooners, bound for Anegada, say.
And it takes other forms. I saw it flickering once
In torches by the railroad tracks in Medellín.
When I was very young I thought that love would come
And seize and take me south and I would see the rose;
And that all ambiguities we knew would merge
Like orchids on a word. Say this:
I sought the immortal word."
                                    So saying he went on
To join those who preceded him;
                            and there were those that followed.

Villanelle at Sundown

Turn your head. Look. The light is turning yellow.
The river seems enriched thereby, not to say deepened.
    Why this is, I'll never be able to tell you.

Or are Americans half in love with failure?
One used to say so, reading Fitzgerald, as it happened.
    (That Viking Portable, all water-spotted and yellow—

Remember?) Or does mere distance lend a value
To things?—false it may be, but the view is hardly cheapened.
    Why this is, I'll never be able to tell you.

The smoke, those tiny cars, the whole urban milieu—
One can like *any*thing diminishment has sharpened.
    Our painter friend, Lang, might show the whole thing yellow

And not be much off. It's nuance that counts, not color—
As in some late James novel, saved up for the long weekend
    And vivid with all the Master simply won't tell you.

How frail our generation has got, how sallow
And pinched with just surviving! We all go off the deep end
    Finally, gold beaten thinly out to yellow.
    And why this is, I'll never be able to tell you.

Nostalgia and Complaint of the Grandparents

Les morts
C'est sous terre;
Ça n'en sort
Guère.
— LAFORGUE

Our diaries squatted, toad-like,
On dark closet ledges.
Forget-me-not and thistle
Decalcomaned the pages.
But where, where are they now,
        All the sad squalors
Of those between-wars parlors?—
Cut flowers; and the sunlight spilt like soda
        On torporous rugs; the photo
Albums all outspread . . .
            The dead
Don't get around much anymore.

There was an hour when daughters
Practiced arpeggios;
Their mothers, awkward and proud,
Would listen, smoothing their hose—
Sundays, half-past five!
        Do you recall
How the sun used to loll,
Lazily, just beyond the roof,
        Bloodshot and aloof?
We thought it would never set.
        The dead don't get
Around much anymore.

Eternity resembles
One long Sunday afternoon.
No traffic passes; the cigar smoke

Curls in a blue cocoon.
Children, have you nothing
        For our cold sakes?
No tea? No little tea cakes?
Sometimes now the rains disturb
    Even our remote suburb.
    There's a dampness underground.
    The dead don't get around
        Much anymore.

Cinema and Ballad of the Great Depression

We men had kept our dignity;
Each wore a cap or a hat. It seemed
We had become a line somehow;
Dark soup was all our dream.

We moved back in with parents. Some days
The awnings creaked like sails.
We lay upstairs on the bedclothes smoking
The long afternoons away.

Sometimes, folding the evening paper up,
One feels suddenly alone.
Yes. And down along the tracks by night
The slow smoke of nomad fires . . .

We slept; and over us a bridge
Arc'd like a promise. To the west
Night-glow of cities always then;
And somebody pulled out a harp.

Pulled a mouth harp out and played,
O lost and wordless . . .
And we were as numerous as leaves;
And some of us turned yellow and some red.

Agriculture embraced Industry,
Mammothly, on public walls.
Meanwhile we camped out underneath
Great smiles on billboards fading.

And home might be some town we passed—
The gingerbread of porches scrolled
In shadow down the white housefronts;
And town boys playing baseball in a road.

Things will go better one day, boys.
Don't ask when.
A decade hence, a war away.
O meet me in the Red Star Mission then!

Pulled out an ancient mouth harp and began to play.

Manhattan Dawn (1945)

There is a smoke of memory
That curls about these chimneys
And then uncurls; that lifts,
Diaphanous, from sleep

To lead us down some alleyway
Still vaguely riverward;
And so at length disperses
Into the wisps and tatters

That garland fire escapes.
—And we have found ourselves again
Watching, beside a misty platform,
The first trucks idling to unload

(New England's frost still
Unstippling down their sides).
                              Or turned
To catch blue truant eyes upon us

Through steam that rose up suddenly from a grate . . .
                              Grinning—
And the grin slid off across the storefronts.
Dawn always seemed to overtake us, though,

Down Hudson somewhere, or Horatio.
—And we have seen it bend
The long stripes of the awnings down
Toward gutters where discarded flowers

Lay washing in the night's small rain—
Hints, glimmerings of a world
Not ours.
          And office towers
Coast among lost stars.

Nostalgia of the Lakefronts

Cities burn behind us; the lake glitters.
A tall loudspeaker is announcing prizes;
Another, by the lake, the times of cruises.
Childhood, once vast with terrors and surprises,
Is fading to a landscape deep with distance—
And always the sad piano in the distance,

Faintly in the distance, a ghostly tinkling
(O indecipherable blurred harmonies)
Or some far horn repeating over water
Its high lost note, cut loose from all harmonies.
At such times, wakeful, a child will dream the world,
And this is the world we run to from the world.

Or the two worlds come together and are one
On dark, sweet afternoons of storm and of rain,
And stereopticons brought out and dusted,
Stacks of old *Geographics*, or, through the rain,
A mad wet dash to the local movie palace
And the shriek, perhaps, of Kane's white cockatoo.
(Would this have been summer, 1942?)

By June the city always seems neurotic.
But lakes are good all summer for reflection,
And ours is famed among painters for its blues,
Yet not entirely sad, upon reflection.
Why sad at all? Is their wish so unique—
To anthropomorphize the inanimate
With a love that masquerades as pure technique?

O art and the child were innocent together!
But landscapes grow abstract, like aging parents.
Soon now the war will shutter the grand hotels,
And we, when we come back, will come as parents.
There are no lanterns now strung between pines—
Only, like history, the stark bare northern pines.

And after a time the lakefront disappears
Into the stubborn verses of its exiles
Or a few gifted sketches of old piers.
It rains perhaps on the other side of the heart;
Then we remember, whether we would or no.
—Nostalgia comes with the smell of rain, you know.

Tremayne

1   THE MILD DESPAIR OF TREMAYNE

Snow melting and the dog
Barks lonely on his bottom from the yard.
The ground is frozen but not hard.

The seasonal and vague
Despairs of February settle over
Tremayne now like a light snow cover,

And he sits thinking; sits
Also not thinking for a while of much.
So February turns to March.

Snow turns to rain; a hyacinth
Pokes up; doves returning moan and sing.
Tremayne takes note of one more spring—

Mordancies of the armchair!—
And finds it hard not to be reconciled
To a despair that seems so mild.

2   THE CONTENTMENT OF TREMAYNE

Tremayne stands in the sunlight,
    Watering his lawn.
The sun seems not to move at all,
    Till it has moved on.

The twilight sounds commence then,
    As those of water cease,
And he goes barefoot through the stir,
    Almost at peace.

Light leans in pale rectangles
    Out against the night.
Tremayne asks nothing more now. There's
    Just enough light,

Or when the street lamp catches
    There should be. He pauses:
How simple it all seems for once!—
    These sidewalks, these still houses.

9   THE INSOMNIA OF TREMAYNE

The all-night stations—Tremayne pictures them
As towers that send great sparks out through the dark—
Fade out and drift among the drifted hours
Just now returning to his bedside clock;
And something starts all over, call it day.
He likes, he really likes the little hum,
Which is the last sound of all night-sounds to decay.

    Call that the static of the spheres, a sound
    Of pure in-betweenness, far, and choked, and thin.
    As long as it lasts—a faint, celestial surf—
    He feels no need to dial the weather in,
    Or music, or the news, or anything.
    And it soothes him, like some night-murmuring nurse,
Murmuring nothing much, perhaps, but murmuring.

4   TREMAYNE AUTUMNAL

Autumn, and a cold rain, and mist,
    In which the dark pine-shapes are drowned,
And taller pole-shapes, and the town lights masked—
A scene, oh, vaguely French Impressionist,
    Tremayne might tell us, if we asked.

Who with his glasses off, half-blind,
    Accomplishes very much the same
Lovely effect of blurs and shimmerings—
Or else October evenings spill a kind
    Of Lethe-water over things.

"O season of half forgetfulness!"
    Tremayne, as usual, misquotes,
Recalling adolescence and old trees
In whose shade once he memorized that verse
    And something about "late flowers for the bees . . ."

Mrs. Snow

Busts of the great composers glimmered in niches,
Pale stars. Poor Mrs. Snow, who could forget her,
Calling the time out in that hushed falsetto?
(How early we begin to grasp what kitsch is!)
But when she loomed above us like an alp,
We little towns below could feel her shadow.
Somehow her nods of approval seemed to matter
More than the stray flakes drifting from her scalp.
Her etchings of ruins, her mass-production Mings
Were our first culture: she put us in awe of things
And once, with her help, I composed a waltz,
Too innocent to be completely false,
Perhaps, but full of marvelous clichés.
She beamed and softened then.

                              Ah, those were the days.

The Pupil

Picture me, the shy pupil at the door,
One small, tight fist clutching the dread Czerny.
Back then time was still harmony, not money,
And I could spend a whole week practicing for
That moment on the threshold.
                                    Then to take courage,
And enter, and pass among mysterious scents,
And sit quite straight, and with a frail confidence
Assault the keyboard with a childish flourish!

Only to lose my place, or forget the key,
And almost doubt the very metronome
(Outside, the traffic, the laborers going home),
And still to bear on across Chopin or Brahms,
Stupid and wild with love equally for the storms
Of C# minor and the calms of C.

The Piano Teachers: A Memoir of the Thirties

So now it is vain for the singer to burst into clamour
With the great black piano appassionato. The glamour
Of childish days is upon me . . .

D.H. LAWRENCE

1   IT WAS A KIND AND NORTHERN FACE:
    MRS. SNOW

Busts of the great composers
Glimmer in niches, pale stars . . .
                    Poor Mrs. Snow!
She towers above her pupils like an alp,
An avalanche threatening sudden
Unasked-for kindnesses.
                    Exiled, alone,
She does not quite complain,
But only sighs and looks off elsewhere,
Regretting the Symphony, perhaps.
                    In dreams, though,
The new palms of the yard,
The one brilliant flame tree
Change back into the elms and maples
Of old, decaying streets.
—Sometimes the inadequate floor quakes
With the effort of her rising.
The great legs, swollen and empurpled,
Can hardly support the hugeness
Of her need.
                    And if
They do not understand—her friends—
She has, in any case, the artistic
Temperament,
                    which isolates—
And saves!
                    Dust motes
Among the Chinese jars. Etchings

Of Greece and Rome. The photograph
Of Mrs. Eddy.

                    Brown sky, so old,
Fading above them all.

   2   BUSTED DREAMS: MRS. L.

                    The faint odour of your patchouli . . .

The mother's flaring skirt
Matches the daughter's.
                    Today
They demonstrate the fox-trot,
Gliding across the living room
And back, each time avoiding
With the same heart-stopping little swoop
                                        or dip
The shabby, cloth-draped, pushed-back, suddenly looming
Sofa.
                    On the piano top,
A nest of souvenirs:
                    paper
Flowers, old programs, a broken fan,
Like a bird's broken wing.
—And sometimes Mr. L. himself
Comes back, recurring, like a dream.
                    He brings
Real flowers. Thin,
Demanding, his voice soars after dark
In the old opera between them.
But no one sees the blows, only
An occasional powdered bruise,
Genteel. Does he come all the way from
Cuba each time for this?
                    The children
Are loosed upon the neighborhood
To wander. In the summer-idle

School yard they are the last ghosts
Of the swings.

                                   Nine o'clock, ten o'clock.
A thousand reconcilings.

                                   The moon . . .

                                   Tomorrow,
On the Havana ferryboat again,
A little over-neat man at the rail,
Examining the waves, his nails.

                                   And she,
Plunging the stiff comb suddenly deep
Into her hair, will turn to greet
Some half-forgotten pupil at the door.

   3   THOSE TROPIC AFTERNOONS: MRS. K.

                                   But in Miami?

Four or five o'clock.

                                   Late summer
Around them like a cocoon,
Gauzy and intimate.
—And sometimes she succumbs
To the passion of a nocturne,
The fury of the climax
Ascending through the folds
Of secret and abandoned flesh
Into those bitten finger-ends
That press from the unsuspecting keys
A certain exaltation—
Only to die away at last
Into a long fermata.
(Satisfaction. The brief
And inward smile.)

                                   Meanwhile,
Dappled with shade of tangelo and mango,

In canvas deck chair that sags,
                        the husband
Sits peering out across
A forlorn sea of half-mown lawn,
Balding, out of work, a sad
Columbus.
                    The drone
Of traffic, far off, reassures:
Fifty-fourth Street still
Leads off toward the Glades at sunset.
                    And the child,
What has he to be afraid of?—
The yellow lesson book
Open on the rack
To that blue, cloudy look of hers?
                    The fan,
Placed on the floor, clicks
With every turn—metronome
Of boredom.
                    Once more, dear: Larghetto.
            Laborers
Coming home, the long day ending.

After-School Practice: A Short Story

Rain that masks the world
Presses it back too hard against
His forehead at the pane.
Three stories down, umbrellas
Are borne along the current of the sidewalk; a bus
Glides like a giant planchette
In some mysterious pattern through the traffic.
Alone now, he feels lost in the new apartment;
He feels some dark cloud shouldering in.
His wish, if he could have one,
Would be for the baby next door to cry out
This minute, signifying end of nap.
Then he could practice. (Apartment life
Is full of these considerations.)
But when finally this does happen,
He still for a time postpones the first chord.
He looks around, full of secrets;
His strange deep thoughts have brought, so far, no harm.
Carefully, with fists and elbows, he prepares
One dark, tremendous chord
Never heard before—his own thunder!
And strikes.
                    And the strings will quiver with it
A long time before the held pedal
Gives up the sound completely—this throbbing
Of the piano's great exposed heart.
Then, soberly, he begins his scales.

And gradually the storm outside dies away also.

The Sunset Maker

*The speaker is a friend of the dead
composer, Eugene Bestor. He is seated on
the terrace of his town house, from which
there is a view of the Gulf of Mexico.*

The Bestor papers have come down to me.
I would suppose, though, they are destined for
The quiet archival twilight of some library.
Meanwhile, I have been sorting scores. The piece
I linger over sometimes is the last,
The "Elegy." So many black, small notes!
They fly above the staff like flags of mourning;
And I can hear the sounds the notes intend.
(Some duo of the mind produces them,
Without error, ghost-music materializing;
Faintly, of course, like whispers overheard.)
And then? I might work up the piano part,
If it mattered. But where is there a cellist
This side of the causeway? And who plays Bestor now?

This time of day I listen to the surf
Myself; I listen to it from my terrace.
The sun eases its way down through the palms,
Scattering colors—a bit of orange, some blues.
Do you know that painting of Bonnard's, *The Terrace*?
It shows a water pitcher blossom-ready
And a woman who bends down to the doomed blossoms—
One of the fates, in orange—and then the sea
With its own streaks of orange, harmonious.
It used to hang in the Phillips near the Steinway.
But who could call back now the web of sound
The cello and the piano made together
In the same Phillips not so long ago?
The three plucked final chords—someone might still
Recall, if not the chords, then the effect

They made—as if the air were troubled somehow.
As if . . . but everything there is is that.
Impressions shimmering; broken light. The world
Is French, if it is anything. Or was.
One phrase the cello had, one early phrase,
That does stay with me, mixed a little now
With Bonnard's colors. A brief rush upward, then
A brief subsiding. Can it be abstract?—
As Stravinsky said it must be to be music.
But what if a phrase *could* represent a thought—
Or feeling, should we say?—without existence
Apart from the score where someone catches it?

Inhale, exhale: a drawn-out gasp or sigh.
Falling asleep, I hear it. It is just there.
I don't say what it means. And I agree
It's sentimental to suppose my friend
Survives in just this fragment, this tone row
A hundred people halfway heard one Sunday
And one of them no more than half remembers.
The hard early years of study, those still,
Sequestered mornings in the studio,
The perfect ear, the technique, the great gift
All have come down to this one ghostly phrase.
And soon nobody will recall the sound
Those six notes made once or that there were six.

Hear the gulls. That's our local music.
I like it myself; and as you can see—
Notice the little orange smudge of the sandbar—
Our sunset maker studied with Bonnard.

From NEW AND SELECTED POEMS

(*1995*)

Orpheus, nothing to look forward to, looked back.
They say he sang then, but the song is lost.
At least he had seen once more the beloved back.

On a Picture by Burchfield

Writhe no more, little flowers. Art keeps long hours.
Already your agony has outlasted ours.

The Artist Orpheus

It was a tropical landscape, much like Florida's, which he knew.
(Childhood came blazing back at him.) They glided across a black
And apathetic river which reflected nothing back
Except his own face sinking gradually from view
As in a fading photograph.
                              Not that he meant to stay,
But, yes, he *would* play something for them, played Ravel;
And sang; and for the first time there were tears in hell.
(Sunset continued. Years passed, or a day.)
And the shades relented finally and seemed sorry.
He could have sworn then he did not look back,
That no one had been following on his track,
Only the thing was that it made a better story
To say that he had heard a sigh perhaps
And once or twice the sound a twig makes when it snaps.

Lorca in California

1 SONG OF THE STATE TROOPERS

Blue are the cycles,
Dark blue the helmets.
The blue sleeves shine
With the rainbows of oil slicks,
And why they don't cry is
Their hearts are leather,
Their skulls are hard plastic.

They come up the roads.
By night they come,
Hunched over headlamps,
Leaving behind them
A silence of rubber
And small fears like beach sand
Ground underheel.
Look, concealed by their helmets
The vague outlines
Of pistols are forming.
They go by—let them pass!

O town of the moonflower,
Preserve of the orange
And the burst guava,
Let them pass!

2 SONG OF THE HOURS

Three cyclists pass under
Christina's window.
How far out she leans!

But tonight she ignores
The flowering goggles.
Tonight she sees nothing
Of fumes, of bandanas.
And the breeze of eight-thirty
Comes fumbling the curtain,
Clumsy, uncertain.
        [Pause: *guitar chord.*]
O, the scent of the lemons!

Two hikers pass under
Christina's window.
How far out she leans!
But tonight she ignores
The bronze of their torsos.
Tonight she hears nothing
Of radios, of sirens.
And the breeze of nine-thirty
Encircles her waist.
How cool it is, how chaste!
        [Pause: *guitar chord.*]
O, the bitter groves!

A young man stands under
Christina's window.
How far out she leans!
But tonight she ignores
The shadow in the shadow.
She sees and hears nothing
But night, the dark night.
And the breeze of ten-thirty
Comes up from the south,
Hot breath on her mouth.
        [Pause: *guitar chord.*]
O, the teeth of their branches!

after Lorca

A Variation on Baudelaire's
"La Servante au grand coeur"

That servant with the big heart but so clumsy—
Remember her?—how objects used to fly
Out of her hands, seized by a sudden whimsy!
And often it would end in a good cry,
Things shattering around her, glass and cup,
Dust where she dusted, spots where she wiped up . . .

She did no real harm, only . . . only
I used to picture her in that cramped room
(The size of a coffin), sinking down in gloom
To wail into her pillow, terribly lonely,
And needing us (we thought) to give some meaning
To her poor life beyond the daily cleaning.

Well, she has gone without us; she has gone
To cross the rivers of the underworld alone.

October's here. It whistles through the orchard.
The leaves blush and are humble at our feet.
So much like Berta—whom we teased and tortured
In childhood all those years.
                            And what if we should meet
Some evening in the shadows of the hall
To find her shrinking back into the wall
Just as she used to, so that we might pass,
Only this time she vanishes like smoke?
And what if some night we dreamed the sound of glass
Breaking, but found no sign of it when we awoke?

*

Three weeks have passed. We should at least have brought
Some flowers for the grave, but no one thought.
Too late, in any case, for she must be
Too wan and hollow-eyed by now to see,
Nor would there be a friend now ever to replace
The worn-out flowers in their little vase.

Invitation to a Ghost

for Henri Coulette (1927–1988)

I ask you to come back now as you were in youth,
Confident, eager, and the silver brushed from your temples.
Let it be as though a man could go backwards through death,
Erasing the years that did not much count,
Or that added up perhaps to no more than a single brilliant
    forenoon.

Sit with us. Let it be as it was in those days
When alcohol brought our tongues the first sweet foretaste of
    oblivion.
And what should we speak of but verse? For who would speak of
    such things now but among friends?
(A bad line, an atrocious line, could make you wince: we have all
    seen it.)

I see you again turn toward the cold and battering sea.
Gull shadows darken the skylight; a wind keens among the chimney
    pots;
Your hand trembles a little.
                  What year was that?

Correct me if I remember it badly,
But was there not a dream, sweet but also terrible,
In which Eurydice, strangely, preceded *you?*
And you followed, knowing exactly what to expect, and of course
    she did turn.

Come back now and help me with these verses.
Whisper to me some beautiful secret that you remember from life.

Vague Memory from Childhood

It was the end of day—
Vast far clouds
In the zenith darkening
    At the end of day.

The voices of my aunts
Sounded through an open window.
Bird-speech cantankerous in a high tree mingled
    With the voices of my aunts.

I was playing alone,
Caught up in a sort of dream,
With sticks and twigs pretending,
    Playing there alone

In the dust.
And a lamp came on indoors,
Printing a frail gold geometry
    On the dust.

Shadows came engulfing
The great charmed sycamore.
It was the end of day.
    Shadows came engulfing.

The Miami of Other Days

[An Improvisation]

The city was not yet itself. It had,
In those days, the simplicity of dawn.
As for the bonfires up and down the beach,
They were nostalgias for the lights of cities
Left behind; and often there would be
Dancing by firelight to the new white jazz
Of a Victrola on its towel in the sand.

Hot afternoons, even the sea breeze sultry
And choking—and underneath the grateful awnings
Of downtown shops the foreign language spoken
With a sound of parrots, excited, incomprehensible;
And crackers down from Georgia (my own people)
Foregathered on the old post office steps,
A sort of club, exchanging news from home;

The winter streets an orchestra of horns . . .

And gods slept under tabernacle tents
That sprang up overnight on circus grounds
Like giant toadstools yearning for respectability,
To be given body by those bell-voiced women
Who blessed in long white sleeves the multitudes;
Or dwelt beneath the still pure river, rising
From time to time, for breath, like great sea cows,
Mysteriously human;
                              and there were sidewalk
Photographers with alligator props
Who disappeared a dozen times a day

Under the black hood of their trade—preservers!
But there was no history, there were only the storms—
And the great bourgeois criminals safely lodged
Under the tiled roofs of the first suburbs,
Living their lives out, bloody and circumspect,
While on quiet corners, in the morning light,
New schools stood humbly waiting for their children.

Nor was the spell that held the city—invisible cloud—
Ever in those days wholly to be lifted.
O "Magic City" of my eighth-grade speech!
Aquarium of the little grounded yacht!
Bandshell of gardenia moons!
And Professor Seward, astronomer, tipping his tall hat
(Like a magician's) nightly to the stars
And to little scatterings of applause still circling maybe
Out there somewhere in the circuits of the lost.

On an Anniversary

Thirty years and more go by
In the blinking of an eye,
    And you are still the same
As when first you took my name.

Much the same blush now as then
Glimmers through the peach-pale skin.
    Time (but as with a glove)
Lightly touches you, my love.

Stand with me a minute still
While night climbs our little hill.
    Below, the lights of cars
Move, and overhead the stars.

The estranging years that come,
Come and go, and we are home.
    Time joins us as a friend,
And the evening has no end.

A Man of 1794

And like a discarded statue, propped up in a cart,
He is borne along toward the page allotted to him in history.

To open his heavy-lidded eyes now would be merely
To familiarize himself with the banal and destined route.

He is aware of the mockery of the streets,
But does not understand it. It hardly occurs to him

That what they fear is that he might yet address them
And call them back to their inflamed duty.

But this he cannot do; the broken jaw prevents speech.
Today he will not accuse the accusers; it is perhaps all that saves
    them.

Meanwhile his head rocks back and forth loosely on his chest
With each new jolt and lurch of the endless-seeming street:

Impossible to resist this idiot shaking.
—But it is hard after all to sympathize

With a man formerly so immaculate,
Who, after a single night of ambiguous confinement,

Lets go all pride of appearance. Nevertheless,
Under the soiled jabot, beneath the stained blue coat,

Are the principles nothing has shaken. Rousseau was right,
Of that he is still convinced: *Man is naturally good!*

And in the moment before the blade eases his pain
He thinks perhaps of his dog or of the woods at Choissy,

Some thought in any case of a perfectly trivial nature,
As though already he were possessed of a sweet, indefinite leisure.

Body and Soul

If there was something one of them held back,
It was too inadvertent or too small
To matter to the other, after all.

Afterwards they were quiet, and lay apart,
And heard the beating of the city's heart,
Meaning the sirens and the street cries, meaning
At dawn, the whispery great street-sweeper cleaning
The things of night up, almost silently.

And all was as it had been and would be.

2   RAIN

The new umbrella, suddenly blowing free,
Escaped across the car hoods dangerously,
And we ran after—
                                        only to be lost
Somewhere along the avenues, long avenues
Toward evening pierced with rain; or down some mews
Whose very cobbles once the young Hart Crane
Had washed with a golden urine mixed with rain.

3 STREET MUSICIAN

A cold evening. The saxophonist shivers
Inside his doorway and ignores the givers
Dropping their change into his upturned hat.
High now or proud, he leans back out of that,
Lifting his horn in some old bluesy riff
His fingers just do manage, being stiff—
Yet so sincere, so naked that it hurts.
Punk teens, in pink hair-spikes and torn T-shirts,
Drift past; a horse-cop towers above the cars;
And office lights wink on in place of stars.

Silence of cities suddenly and the snow
Turning to rain and back again to snow . . .

On a Woman of Spirit Who Taught
Both Piano and Dance

Thanks to the Powers-
That-Once-Were for her rouges
And powders, those small cosmetic subterfuges
Which were the gloss upon her book of hours;
And to Madam L. herself, whose heart
Was a hummingbird, and flew from art to art.

Dance Lessons of the Thirties

Wafts of old incense mixed with Cuban coffee
Hung on the air; a fan turned; it was summer.
And (of the buried life) some last aroma
Still clung to the tumbled cushions of the sofa.

At lesson time, pushed back, it used to be
The thing we managed somehow just to miss
With our last-second dips and whirls—all this
While the Victrola wound down gradually.

And this was their exile, those brave ladies who taught us
So much of art, and stepped off to their doom
Demonstrating the fox-trot with their daughters
Endlessly around some sad and makeshift ballroom.

O little lost Bohemias of the suburbs!

Banjo Dog Variations

Tramps on the road: floating clouds.
—OLD CHINESE POEM

1

Agriculture and Industry
Embraced in public on a wall—
Heroes in shirt-sleeves! Next to them
The average man felt small.

2

I dreamed I saw Joe Hill last night,
By Vassar girls surrounded.
They harmonized expertly; oh,
Their little true hearts pounded.

Joe went on smiling.

3

I thought I saw what Trotsky saw,
A friendly cossack wink;
And then his friends brought down their clubs.
Christ, what would Trotsky think!

4

Train had just slowed for the crossing when
Out from the bushes jumped a hundred men.
With baseball bats and iron bars
They persuaded us back onto the cars.

5

And out of dirty fists sometimes
Would bloom the melancholy harp.
Then low-low-low on the gon-doh-lah
We swayed beneath our tarp.

And far lights moving in and out of rain.

6

What you do with the Sunday news
Oh, citizens of the great riffraff,
Is you put the funny papers in your shoes.
It gives the feet a laugh.

7

We read our brothers' shirts for lice
And moved around with the fruit,
Went north to Billings for the beets
And had three good days in the jail at Butte.

8

We chalked our names on red cliffsides,
High up, where only eagles dwelled.
Each time a big truck went by below
The earth trembled like a woman held.

9

And we passed fields of smoking stumps
Where goats sometimes or ponies grazed.
Abandoned tractors stood against the sky
Like giant fists upraised.

10

But if we bent our knees it was
To drink from a creek's rust-colored slime,
And splash our chests with it, and rub our eyes,
And wake into another world and time.

11

Let us go then, you and me,
While the neon bubbles upward ceaselessly
To lure us down back streets and alleyways,
Where we may wander and be lost for days.

Many days and many hours.

12

I miss the smell of ratty furs
And Saturday night cologne and beer,
And I miss the juke and the sign that read:
NO POLICE SERVED HERE.

13

Off Mission, wasn't it? The old
White Angel Breadline, where we met?
You had just come west from Arkansas,
But the rest of it I forget.

A cup of coffee; afterwards a hymn.

14

Once we stood on a high bluff,
Lights fanning out across the bay.
A little ragged band of Christs we were,
And tempted—but we turned away.

15

And didn't I see you Saturday night,
After the paycheck from the mill,
Bearing a pot of store-bought lilies home,
One budding still?

Ah, oh, my banjo dog!

Pantoum of the Great Depression

Our lives avoided tragedy
Simply by going on and on,
Without end and with little apparent meaning.
Oh, there were storms and small catastrophes.

Simply by going on and on
We managed. No need for the heroic.
Oh, there were storms and small catastrophes.
I don't remember all the particulars.

We managed. No need for the heroic.
There were the usual celebrations, the usual sorrows.
I don't remember all the particulars.
Across the fence, the neighbors were our chorus.

There were the usual celebrations, the usual sorrows.
Thank god no one said anything in verse.
The neighbors were our only chorus,
And if we suffered we kept quiet about it.

At no time did anyone say anything in verse.
It was the ordinary pities and fears consumed us,
And if we suffered we kept quiet about it.
No audience would ever know our story.

It was the ordinary pities and fears consumed us.
We gathered on porches; the moon rose; we were poor.
What audience would ever know our story?
Beyond our windows shone the actual world.

We gathered on porches; the moon rose; we were poor.
And time went by, drawn by slow horses.
Somewhere beyond our windows shone the world.
The Great Depression had entered our souls like fog.

And time went by, drawn by slow horses.
We did not ourselves know what the end was.
The Great Depression had entered our souls like fog.
We had our flaws, perhaps a few private virtues.

But we did not ourselves know what the end was.
People like us simply go on.
We have our flaws, perhaps a few private virtues,
But it is by blind chance only that we escape tragedy.

And there is no plot in that; it is devoid of poetry.

Sadness

Dear ghosts, dear presences, O my dear parents,
Why were you so sad on porches, whispering?
What great melancholies were loosed among our swings!
As before a storm one hears the leaves whispering
    And marks each small change in the atmosphere,
    So was it then to overhear and to fear.

But all things then were oracle and secret.
Remember the night when, lost, returning, we turned back
Confused, and our headlights singled out the fox?
Our thoughts went with it then, turning and turning back
    With the same terror, into the deep thicket
    Beside the highway, at home in the dark thicket.

I say the wood within is the dark wood,
Or wound no torn shirt can entirely bandage,
But the sad hand returns to it in secret
Repeatedly, encouraging the bandage
    To speak of that other world we might have borne,
    The lost world buried before it could be born.

4

Burchfield describes the pinched white souls of violets
Frothing the mouth of a derelict old mine
Just as an evil August night comes down,
All umber, but for one smudge of dusky carmine.
    It is the sky of a peculiar sadness—
    The other side perhaps of some rare gladness.

5

What is it to be happy, after all? Think
Of the first small joys. Think of how our parents
Would whistle as they packed for the long summers,
Or, busy about the usual tasks of parents,
    Smile down at us suddenly for some secret reason,
    Or simply smile, not needing any reason.

6

But even in the summers we remember
The forest had its eyes, the sea its voices,
And there were roads no map would ever master,
Lost roads and moonless nights and ancient voices—
    And night crept down with an awful slowness toward the water;
    And there were lanterns once, doubled in the water.

7

Sadness has its own beauty, of course. Toward dusk,
Let us say, the river darkens and looks bruised,
And we stand looking out at it through rain.
It is as if life itself were somehow bruised
    And tender at this hour; and a few tears commence.
    Not that they *are* but that they *feel* immense.

NEW POEMS

Epitaph for a Pair of Old Shoes

Humble, born to the earth,
They knew where they stood.

When they moved,
It was because they must.

Anger moved them,
And the desire to be elsewhere,

Or something in them
Responding to music.

They knew also
What waiting can be.

Side by side, they mastered it,
Like an old married couple.

"Sonya sits at the piano, practicing"

1

Sonya sits at the piano, practicing.
She yearns for what does not exist, it seems,
Something beyond all music; and to her
The whole pathos of chromaticism seems
      A purely mechanical exercise.
      And yet she sighs and does not know why she sighs.

2

So at reunions, recognizing the songs,
We feel at one with the sadness of our class.
The singing spreads, spreads and becomes general—
O ineluctable blues of the middle class!
      Softly we sing, and the more forgetful hum.
      Time the River, Time the Destroyer! Yes, ho hum.

3

Glorious to be away from the mill at last!
On such a day the sky looks strangely poetic
With all the sad poetry of chimney and of gable.
To the young poet, of course, everything looks poetic—
      The clouds, the vast white Saturday afternoon,
      Yes, even the grimy mill-men tavern-bound at noon.

The Voice of Col. von Stauffenberg Ascending
Through the Smoke and Dull Flames of Purgatory

Something dreadful has happened. . . . The
Führer is alive!
—GEN. FELLGIEBEL, JULY 20, 1944

Our last night we passed quietly, my brother and I;
Sat talking of poems into the small hours.

And saw, toward dawn, for the last time, through the beautiful tall
    windows,
The smoke as of some great sacrifice suspended over the city.

And the little life remaining seemed very full.

Ah, but to turn away then, to turn one's back to God,
To cast oneself aside as simply as a child
Discards the doll he has grown weary of . . .

They led us out that evening into the courtyard.
There was a mound of earth there, left from the excavations;

Against this they posed us.
And it was there that the lights of the parked cars found us—

So all it had come to in the end was sorrow only,
Sorrow, and the overwhelming regret
That through failure one had been spared for heaven after all.

Ralph: A Love Story

In the early days of cinema the stars did not yet have names.

In what had been a failing music store
A man named Flowers opened the first cinema
In Moultrie. Ralph was the projectionist,
At seventeen the first projectionist.
There was an old upright from the store
On which the wife accompanied the action
With little bursts of von Suppé and Wagner.

Ralph liked the dark of the projection booth;
He liked the flickering images on the screen.
And yet because he liked it all so well,
He feared expulsion from this little Eden,
Not so much feared as knew the day must come,
Given his luck, when it would all run out,
Which made the days more paradisal still.

Margot, the daughter, twenty and unmarried—
To tell it all quickly—seduced Ralph.
She let him think he was seducing her.
They used to meet in the projection booth,
Embracing wordlessly but laughing too,
Unable to suppress their self-delight.
Time after time they had been almost caught.
Then, as in novels, Margot became pregnant.

Sundays the cinema was closed. Ralph packed
And slipped off to the depot about dusk.
That evening from the train he watched with a certain nostalgia
The sparse pale farmlights passing from his life—

And he understood nothing, only that he was young.
Within a week or two he had joined the navy.

Not that he realized it at the time,
But those quick laughing grapplings in the dark
Would be the great romance his life would know,
Though there would be more women, more than he wanted
Really, before it was all finished for him.
And even in the last few years, working
His final job, night watchman at a warehouse,
He might be resting on a stack of lumber,
Toward morning, say, and there would come to him
The faces of the stars before the stars
Had names, only dark-painted eyes, and hands
That spoke the sign-language of the secret heart.
(Oh, not that he remembered. He did not.)

She wrote him over the first months two letters
In care of his parents in another town.
The envelopes were decorated boldly
With home-drawn hearts, some broken, pierced by arrows.
The mother must have guessed the truth and thought
To spare the son by keeping back the letters
Until the time seemed ripe for him to have them.
And when his tour of duty ended finally
He did unseal and read them and was sorry.
But he could not go back to it, he could not.

So it was gone, the way a thing will go
Yet keep a sort of phantom presence always.
He might be drinking with some woman, lying
Beside her on a tourist cabin bed,
When something would come ghosting back to him,
Some little thing. Such paradise it had been!

And when it *was* all finished for him, at the end,
In the small bedroom of his sister's house,

Surrounded by his shelves of paperbacks—
Westerns mostly, and a few private-eyes—
Lying there on the single bed, half gone
On Echo Springs, he could not call it back.
Or if it came back it was in the form
Of images in the dark, shifting and flashing,
Badly projected, spooling out crazily
In darkness, in a little room, and he
Could not control it. It was like dying.
No, it *was* dying, and he let it go.

Couplets Concerning Time

1

Have I not waited with a numbed impatience
In polite pale rooms with polite anonymous patients?

2

The auctioneer lifts his gavel: *Going! Going!*
Whence come we, what are we, whither are we going?

3

The procession turns up the lane. The young poet watches.
Time enters his head—the tick of a thousand watches.

4

The years stand lonely on their sidings now like abandoned cars,
The wind in the wires and snow sifting down on the cars.

5

The clouds, the vast white Saturday afternoon,
And the high mournful whistle crying, *Noooon, Noooon.*

At the Young Composers' Concert

Sewanee, Tennessee, summer, 1996

The melancholy of these young composers
Impresses me. There will be time for joy.

Meanwhile, one can't help noticing the boy
Who bends down to his violin as if

To comfort it in its precocious grief.
It is his composition, confused and sad,

Made out of feelings he has not yet had
But only caught some hint or rumor of

In the old scores—and that has been enough.
Merely mechanical, sure, all artifice—

But can that matter when it sounds like this?
What matters is the beauty of the attempt,

The world for him being so far mostly dreamt.
Not that a lot, to tell the truth, has passed,

Nothing to change our lives or that will last.
And not that we are awed, exactly; still,

There is something *to* this beyond mere adult skill.
And if it moves but haltingly down the scales,

It is the more moving just because it fails;
And is the lovelier because we know

It has gone beyond itself, as great things go.

School Letting Out

(Fourth or Fifth Grade)

The afternoons of going home from school
Past the young fruit trees and the winter flowers.
The schoolyard cries fading behind you then,
And small boys running to catch up, as though
It were an honor somehow to be near—
All is forgiven now, even the dogs,
Who, straining at their tethers, used to bark,
Not from anger but some secret joy.

The Small White Churches of the Small White Towns

The twangy, off-key hymn songs of the poor,
Not musical, but somehow beautiful.
And the paper fans in motion, like little wings.

A Chapter in the Life of Mr. Kehoe, Fisherman

Some nights on the dock,
When only scales
And a few pop-eyed fish-heads
Are left out for the moon
(Which the spread nets entangle),
There comes a sound
Of bare feet dancing,
Which is Mr. Kehoe,
Lindying solo,
Whirling, dipping,
In his long skirt
That swells and billows,
Turquoise and pink,
Mr. Kehoe in sequins,
Face tilted moonward,
Eyes half-shut, dreaming.

Sleep well, Mr. Kehoe.

"There is a gold light in certain old paintings"

1

There is a gold light in certain old paintings
That represents a diffusion of sunlight.
It is like happiness, when we are happy.
It comes from everywhere and from nowhere at once, this light,
     And the poor soldiers sprawled at the foot of the cross
     Share in its charity equally with the cross.

2

Orpheus hesitated beside the black river.
With so much to look forward to he looked back.
We think he sang then, but the song is lost.
At least he had seen once more the beloved back.
     I say the song went this way: *O prolong*
     Now the sorrow if that is all there is to prolong.

3

The world is very dusty, uncle. Let us work.
One day the sickness shall pass from the earth for good.
The orchard will bloom; someone will play the guitar.
Our work will be seen as strong and clean and good.
     And all that we suffered through having existed
     Shall be forgotten as though it had never existed.

Notes

With only one exception, the order of the poems here follows their order in the original volumes. I have generally used the most recent published version of each poem, though here and there I have altered a word or a phrase. Where the most recent version no longer pleased me, I have gone back to an earlier version. I would like to thank Deborah Garrison, Ilana Kurshan, and William Logan for their kind help. They have made easier a task that the ailments of my age have made more difficult.

"On a Painting by Patient B of the Independence State Hospital for the Insane": B's names for the clouds were Rabbit, Bear, and Hyena. The town depicted in his painting he called Beverly Hills. Independence is in Iowa.

Don Juan in Hell was to have been a puppet opera, based on the Baudelaire poem.

"The Metamorphoses of a Vampire": Line 12 of the French text I was using reads *véloutés* rather than *rédoutés*.

"Bad Dreams": The unfinished long poem from which these three pieces come was to have been made up mostly of dreams dreamed by the kinspeople gathered in the house of the family patriarch on the night he lies dying. Some debt for the idea is doubtless owed to James Agee and Peter Taylor, but I can no longer judge how much.

"Incident in a Rose Garden": The Somerset Maugham version of this legend, used by John O'Hara as the epigraph for his *Appointment in Samarra*, goes as follows:

> DEATH SPEAKS: *There was a merchant in Bagdad who sent his servant to market to buy provisions and in a little while the servant came back, white and trembling, and said, Master, just now when I was in the market-place I was jostled by a woman in the crowd and when I turned I saw it was Death that jostled me. She looked at me and made a threatening gesture; now, lend me your horse, and I will ride away from this city and avoid my fate. I will go to Samarra and there Death will not find me. The merchant lent him his horse, and the servant mounted it, and he dug his spurs in its flanks and as fast as the horse could gallop he went. Then the merchant went down to the market-place and he saw me standing in the*

crowd and he came to me and said, Why did you make a threatening gesture to my servant when you saw him this morning? That was not a threatening gesture, I said, it was only a start of surprise. I was astonished to see him in Bagdad, for I had an appointment with him tonight in Samarra.

"ABC": Some images in the "B" section are adapted from a series of poems by Guillevic (*Choses*).

"A Dancer's Life": Most of the details were remembered, perhaps wrongly, from early Bergman movies, scripts, and criticism.

"On the Night of the Departure by Bus" and "Cool Dark Ode" (of "Three Odes") are loosely modeled in structure on poems by Rafael Alberti. See "En el día de su muerte a mano armada" and the fourth part of "Colegio (S.J.)." Several lines in "White Notes" were also suggested by passages scattered throughout his *Sobre los ángeles*.

"The Confession," "The Success," "The Assassination," and, to some extent, the sonatinas ("Sonatina in Green" and "Sonatina in Yellow") come in part from chance methods.

"1971" is a departure from a translation by John Batki of Attila József.

The remote sources for "After the Chinese" (in "From a Notebook") appear in *The Penguin Book of Chinese Verse* (Yang Wan-Li, Wang Chia, Ch'in Chia, and Chĕng-Yen).

"Riddle" is based on a well-known Old English riddle.

"Variations on a Text by Vallejo": The Greek poet Kostas Ouránis (1890–1953) deserves some credit for this motif. Though I did not come across it until years after my own version, Ouránis has a poem apparently dating from 1915, the first line of which, in Kimon Friar's translation, reads: "I shall die one day on a mournful autumn twilight."

"Homage to the Memory of Wallace Stevens": The last section refers to a libretto I wrote for Edward Miller's opera *The Young God,* to its performance, and to the accompanying celebrations, which took place in Hartford in the spring of 1969. Avon is a suburb of Hartford. Line 22 is intended to echo a famous line from *Lycidas.*

"Memories of the Depression Years": The second section (Boston, Georgia) is a kind of *imitation* of a Wang Wei poem, which has been translated as "A Farmhouse on the Wei River." The third section (Miami, Florida) bears a similar relation to Baudelaire's *Je n'ai pas oublié.*

"Childhood": Line 2: Czechoslovakia, for example. Line 5: *The Katzenjammer Kids* was for years the feature comic strip of the Sunday *Miami Herald*. Lines 23–26: The Olympia Theater, now the Gusman Center for the Performing Arts. Lines 32ff.: The hurricane season. Line 37: An obsolete make of car. Lines 38–39: The Everglades on fire. Lines 40ff.: My osteomyelitis and the anesthesias it involved. Lines 44–45: The Capitol Barber Shop, Miami Avenue. Lines 46–47: Billy's Men's Shop. Lines 49–50: In Cromer-Cassell's (later Richards') Department Store. Line 52: The segregated drinking fountains of those days. Lines 54ff.: The 5-and-10-cent stores. A tray of unsorted eyeglasses at Grant's. A toy display in Woolworth's. Lines 58ff.: The N.W. section, still under development. Line 69: Sunny Isles, Golden Glades, Buena Vista, Opa-Locka, etc.

"American Scenes (1904–1905)": The first section is pieced together from the *Notebooks*, the second and third sections from *American Scenes*. In California, James stayed at the famous Hotel del Coronado near San Diego.

"Nineteenth-Century Portrait": See Baudelaire's "A une Malabaraise." I have shifted the scene from Malabar and Paris to the Caribbean and New York. Richard Howard's translation provided the hibiscus.

"Young Girls Growing Up (1911)": See *The Diaries of Franz Kafka: 1910–1913*, entries for November 29 and December 3.

"Sea Wind: A Song" and "Last Evening: At the Piano" both date from Rilke's stay in Capri early in 1907. My versions came out of an attempt to write a play based loosely on that period in Rilke's life. The famous image of the death's-head shako with which "Letzer Abend" ends I have de-Prussianized, since in my play both poet and setting had become American. See "Lied vom Meer (Capri, Piccola Marina)" and "Letzer Abend."

"Hell": Line 6 is taken unchanged from "The Spell," a poem in Robert Boardman Vaughn's unpublished ms. Parts of the next few lines are freely adapted from another poem of his, "The Black Rose."

"The Sunset Maker": The musical quotation comes from a piece I wrote as a student of Carl Ruggles in 1943.

"Lorca in California": From a journal: "July 17, 1974: Idea for a play. Death of a poet. Lorca in California. Time: 1999. Reagan has been governor for generations. Orange groves, guitars, motorcycles." The adaptations are of two well-known poems of Lorca's, "Romance de la Guardia Civil Española" and "Arbolé, arbolé."

Index of Titles

Index of First Lines

About the Author

Donald Justice was born in Miami, Florida, in 1925 and grew up there. After graduating from the University of Miami, where he studied musical composition, he attended the universities of North Carolina, Stanford, and Iowa. He taught at several universities, chiefly at the University of Iowa and at the University of Florida. He was the author of numerous books and the recipient of many grants and prizes, including the Pulitzer Prize for his *Selected Poems* (1979). He lived with his wife in Iowa City until his death in August 2004.

A Note on the Type

This book was set in a type called Baskerville. The face itself is a facsimile reproduction of types cast from the molds made for John Baskerville (1706–1775) from his designs. Baskerville's original face was one of the forerunners of the type style known to printers as "modern face"—a "modern" of the period A.D. 1800.

Composed by NK Graphics, Keene, New Hampshire
Printed and bound by Berryville Graphics, Berryville, Virginia
Designed by Anthea Lingeman